Savannah's Garden Plants

Roy Heizer
Photography by Nancy Heizer

Schiffer Publishing Ltd®

4880 Lower Valley Road, Atglen, Pennsylvania 19310

Dedication

This book is dedicated to Charles H. Keiser, D.V.M. and
Paul Thompson, my first horticultural mentors.

Schiffer Books are available at special discounts for bulk purchases for sales promotions or premiums. Special editions, including personalized covers, corporate imprints, and excerpts can be created in large quantities for special needs. For more information contact the publisher:
Published by Schiffer Publishing Ltd.
4880 Lower Valley Road
Atglen, PA 19310
Phone: (610) 593-1777; Fax: (610) 593-2002
E-mail: Info@schifferbooks.com

For the largest selection of fine reference books on this and related subjects, please visit our web site at www.schifferbooks.com
We are always looking for people to write books on new and related subjects. If you have an idea for a book please contact us at the above address.

This book may be purchased from the publisher. Include $5.00 for shipping. Please try your bookstore first. You may write for a free catalog.

In Europe, Schiffer books are distributed by
Bushwood Books,
6 Marksbury Ave.
Kew Gardens
Surrey TW9 4JF England
Phone: 44 (0) 20 8392 8585; Fax: 44 (0) 20 8392 9876
E-mail: info@bushwoodbooks.co.uk
Website: www.bushwoodbooks.co.uk

Other Schiffer Books on Related Subjects:
The Art of the Garden: Collecting Antique Botanical Prints. Denise DeLaurentis & Hollie Powers Holt. ISBN: 0-7643-2407-1. $79.95
Today's Botanical Artists. Cora Marcus & Libby Kyer. ISBN: 978-0-7643-2905-0. $39.95

Copyright © 2009 by Roy Heizer
Photographs © 2009 by Nancy Heizer

Library of Congress Control Number: 2009931423

Designed by Mark David Bowyer
Type set in Aldine 721 BT / Zurich BT

ISBN: 978-0-7643-3265-4
Printed in China

Contents

Tibochiana

Acknowledgments

I thank my friends and family for their support of this project:

Everyone at Schiffer Publishing

Susan Jaffie at Smooth, a smoothie, coffee, and internet café on Bull Street, between Wright and Chippewa Squares in Savannah's Historic District

The Owens-Thomas House and Gardens

The Juliette Gordon Low Birthplace House and Gardens

The Mercer Williams House and Gardens

Stan Gray with "The Rainbow Goddess Collection", an Iris collection on display at The Bamboo Farm and Coastal Gardens

The Garden Club of Savannah at The Savannah Botanical Garden

The Master Gardeners of Savannah

The Bamboo Farm and Coastal Garden, a public research farm and division of the University of Georgia

Dr. Charles H. Keiser, D.V.M., owner of Blue Heron Acres tree farm in Danville, Kentucky

Paul Thompson, Extension agent with Clemson University in York Co. South Carolina.

Folklorico, Folk and Indigenous Art, 14 W. Jones St., Savannah

Michael Jordan of the Georgia Coastal Heritage Society

Four Seasons Garden Center, Savannah, Georgia

Savannah Chamber of Commerce

The North Carolina Nursery and Landscape Assn.

The South Carolina Nursery and Landscape Assn.

The Georgia Green Industry

Bob Calabrese

Introduction

ℐ beautiful and historic seaport city, Savannah is truly a gardener's paradise. Enjoy and explore the history, folklore and science for some of America's most wonderful garden and landscape plants. Learn why a Georgia shipwright would have grown the Live Oak, and what makes the Mulberry tree special in Savannah's history. Find out how wine and ivy are intertwined, and which landscape plants are traditionally used in religious services. Read the story of the flowers, plants and trees that grow in and around Savannah.

The book is arranged by the plants' botanical names in alphabetical order to be reader friendly, with clear color photographs that were taken in their natural environment using natural light. Because the photographs were not staged, they can be appreciated as the gardener would see them. The book takes readers beyond the average gardening experience to see flowers and landscape trees from a wider perspective, all the while having the fun that drew gardeners to the plants in the first place. Also, you will learn new facts and folklore to pass on to your friends.

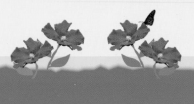

The Plants

arranged alphabetically by their botanical name

S avannah is a garden. All of the plants featured in this guidebook can be found growing in and around the Savannah area and are open to the public. As you stroll through Savannah, keep your eyes open and you will quickly realize flowers, plants, and trees are everywhere. From rooftop terraces to open alleys, from formal English gardens and window boxes to massive Live Oak trees and flowering shrubs, every season in Savannah holds unique surprises for the gardener.

Abutilon ✓
Flowering Maple or Tomochichi's Lantern

Abutilon, or Flowering Maple, is native to South and Central America. This is where, for centuries, it has been used by Native American tribes for its warm, almost glowing flower. Abutilon flowers are said to be the color of flames with brilliant reds, oranges, yellows and whites. There are many South American stories surrounding this flower, but it is a uniquely Georgian story that speaks most eloquently of this flower to Savannah gardeners.

Abutilon

It was here in Savannah in 1733, on a bluff overlooking the river, that Tomochichi greeted Oglethorpe and the first Georgia colonists. Legend has it that Tomochichi carried a stave of Abutilon with a magnificent set of arching lantern like flowers at the top. With his glorious lantern of flowers casting light upon the darkness and uncertainty of the wilderness, Tomochichi's lantern lit the way of friendship between the Yamacraw and the Colonial settlers. Years later, at Tomochichi's funeral, the Savannah colonists carried Abutilon flowers to show that the way of friendship was still being lit by Tomochichi's Lantern.

White

Acanthus
Acanthus or Bear's Breeches

Bearing a beautiful flower spike and a distinctive leaf, Acanthus is both a historical and mythical plant in Greek and Roman cultures. In ancient Greece and Rome, the Acanthus leaf was used as an architectural feature. It was used as an adornment on Corinthian columns and pedestal ornaments.

Acanthus

Acanthus leaves continue to be used today in Greek style architecture. Bear's Breeches are still a standard decorating motif today, found in wallpaper, fabrics, paintings, corbels and landscapes.

Acanthus leaves and flowers also have many mythological stories associated with them. Acantha, a nymph in Greek mythology, was loved by Apollo, the sun god. In one version of their story, Apollo turned her into an Acanthus plant after she refused his advances and scratched his face when he tried to seduce her. Apollo forever doomed her to be a beautiful flower, but full of thorns.

A confusing aspect of the Acantha mythological story is that the Acanthus is a shrub and that nymphs, as tree fairies, would not have been associated with a shrub.

Acer Palmatum
Japanese Red Maple

Japanese Red Maples, along with Crape Myrtles, provide locals with their best autumn color. It is also popular with Bonsai

enthusiasts and has been widely used throughout the history of that art.

Japanese Red Maples were first developed from regular sized Maples to be used as Bonsai plants.

In fact the word Bonsai means "Little Tree" in both the Chinese and Japanese languages. Japanese Red Maple lovers have many different cultivars from which to choose.

Acer Palmatum

Achillea
Yarrow or Soldiers' Woundwort

The botanical name Achillea comes from a Greek mythological character, Achilles. The legend says that Achilles carried Yarrow in times of war to treat his soldiers' battle wounds. Hence, Yarrow got the common name Soldiers' Woundwort. It was said that Achilles body was invincible, except for one spot, his heel. One night during the Trojan War, Achilles did not have any Yarrow with him when he was struck in the heel by an arrow, killing him. As the legend goes, Achilles perished because he neglected to carry Yarrow to sooth his wound. It is due to Achilles and the legend of the Yarrow that we have the saying "Achilles' heel", meaning a weak or vulnerable spot.

Achillea

Agapanthus Africanus
Agapanthus, Plum Plum or Lily of Good Hope

Agapanthus is a wonderful garden plant in Savannah. It lights up the border in May, just as the Azaleas are fading. Blue is the Agapanthus color that is most widely planted, although a bright white is grown as well. The sky doesn't want competition, so blue is the least available flower color in nature, making

the blue of the Agapanthus a treasured favorite. Agapanthus is sometimes mistakenly called Lily of the Nile, after the Nile River in Northern Africa. Lily of Good Hope is actually native to South Africa, along the Cape of Good Hope. In South Africa, it is often called Plum Plum.

Agapanthus

Agastache
Hyssop or Butterfly Mint

Agastache is a wonderful garden flower for the Savannah landscape. It attracts butterflies and bees with its late spring blossoms. The flowers are usually white, pink, purple or salmon, with the bracts that come behind the flowers often being a slightly contrasting color. A reliable perennial in Savannah gardens, this Mint and Salvia relative can be enjoyed year after year. Butterfly Mint can be divided in the spring or fall and given to friends.

Agastache

Agave
Century Plant or American Aloe

A Century Plant, the centerpiece of the Juliette Gordon Low Birthplace house museum garden, is one of the largest landscape plants grown in Savannah. Juliette Gordon Low is the founder of the Girl Scouts of America. The Girl Scouts of America continue to preserve this house museum in her honor.

Native to Mexico, Agave has historically been harvested for everything from Tequila to fibers strong enough to be used as thread. In America it is enjoyed as a fascinating plant that flowers infrequently, about once every seventy -five years, hence the name Century Plant.

It is also called the American Aloe, although it is not a true Aloe. In Greek mythology, Agave was the daughter of Cadmus and the goddess Harmonia. Cadmus was the king and founder of the city of Thebes, Greece.

Agave

Albizia Julibrissin
Mimosa Tree, Tree of Beauty and Perseverance

This widely grown, tropical looking tree is a staple in Savannah gardens. Gardener's either cultivate or eradicate them. This dueling nature is how Mimosa became known in nature stories as the Tree of Beauty and Perseverance.

The Mimosa has arching graceful branches that produce small leaflets along with puffy, soft pink flowers that look like pom-poms, giving it a Caribbean island feel. Its summer beauty is almost unmatched as it sways in the wind. A natural habitat for birds, butterflies and squirrels, it is a wonder for the tree or animal enthusiast. But, it seeds quite profusely and is also a tenacious grower that sometimes comes up where it is not wanted. Once established in a given area it is difficult to remove. The Mimosa Tree likes its status along the fine line between beauty and perseverance.

In its native Persia, or modern day Iran, there is a story of how Mimosa Tree flowers were used to adorn the palace and crowns of a Persian king and his beautiful queen. The king was strong and powerful, yet gentle. The queen was well known for her unparalleled beauty and compassion. The king and queen were wildly popular with their people and so they planted Mimosa Trees all over Persia as a tribute to him and a sign of respect for her. The Mimosa Tree, known even then for its beauty and perseverance, became an ancient symbol for the Persian Empire's strength and vibrant culture.

Albizia

Aloe
Aloe

Aloe is well known for its medicinal properties. It can be found as well in many skin care products. It has been used for centuries as a wound and sunburn salve, and can be applied as a gel. Cleopatra was even said to have used it as a beauty aid. In ancient Egypt it was also used as an embalming ingredient.

Aloe, native to all of Africa, is therefore found in South Africa's Cape Province. It is common in the islands off the African coast, such as Madagascar, and in the Arabian peninsula.

Aloe is also a beautiful garden plant, producing wonderful spikes of salmon, red or yellow flowers. It is easy to grow in the Savannah garden border when planted in full sun and left a little dry once established.

Aloe

Alstroemeria
Princess Lily, Inca Lily or Lily of the Incas

An Inca legend says that the Princess Lily was the favorite flower of the daughter of the Incan leader, Manco Capac. As Capac expanded and spread the Incan empire across South America, his daughter and the Princess Lily went with him. Capac was said to be a tenacious and resilient leader who adopted the Inca Lily as his symbol. Capac used the Lily of the Incas not only because it was his daughter's favorite, but because of this flower's tenacious, spreading qualities that reminded him of the Incan Empire itself.

A fascinating morphological trait of Alstroemeria and its relatives is the fact that the leaves are resupinate. The leaves twist from the base so that what appears to be the upper leaf surface is in fact the lower leaf surface. This very unusual trait is easily observed in the Savannah garden or on the leaves of cut flowers that can be found in floral shops.

Alstroemeria

Alstroemeria

Animagiqualmicus Imaginariensis
Animaginary

Although this plant is completely a figment of the author's imagination, you can see it growing in several spots around Savannah. Animaginary trees are thought to be a hybrid between Live Oaks and Sabal Palmettos, but, because they do not exist, scientists have so far been unable to confirm this.

While a copycat tree, the Oalm, has been spotted in Bonaventure Cemetery, the pictured Animaginary tree can be seen in LaFayette Square.

Animagiqualmicus

Antirrhinum
Snapdragons or Motley Mouth

Antirrhinum is a family of flowering plants more commonly known as snapdragon, because this flower resembles the head of a dragon. When snapdragon flowers are squeezed, they snap open and closed, like the mouth of a dragon.

Antirrhinum gets its other common name, motley mouth, due to the fact that this Southern favorite comes in many colors. Motley mouth is sold in the North as an annual, but here in Savannah it is a self-seeding perennial.

Antirrhinum

Asclepias Tuberosa
Butterfly Weed or Indian Paintbrush

Asclepius Tuberosa

Because of the color and large production of nectar, butterflies are attracted to this perennial's flower, hence the common name. Butterfly weed is also the food plant of the Queen butterfly while in the larva stage. The Butterfly weed flowers in Savannah from the middle of May into November.

The other common name, Indian Paintbrush, comes from an old Native American folklore tale about how the Indians once used its brightly colored flowers to paint their horses, tents and faces with their tribal colors in the summer.

Aspidistra Elatior
Cast Iron Plant

Looking for the perfect evergreen perennial? Cast Iron Plant may be the perfect choice. It looks great year round when planted outside in a part sun to part shade location, and with very little watering. If Cast Iron Plant is planted in a spot that gets rain water, it will never need to be hand watered. The only real downside to Cast Iron Plant is that it does not flower; however, it is an outstanding large leafed foliage plant. As a house plant, it needs water only once a month and, unlike many houseplants, Cast Iron Plant is ignored by cats.

Aspidistra Elatior

Aucuba
Gold Dust Plant or Spotted Laurel

Aucuba

Gold Dust Plant is originally from Japan, but it is a story from California that tells of the Aucuba's journey across America. It was in California, in 1849, that America had a gold rush that sent many men out west. Meanwhile, the families of these men waited back east for them to return with loads of gold. Many of these men from the east spent several disappointing months panning for gold in the California mountains. Most of the men were able to pan amounts of gold that could only be described as "dust."

Not wanting to return home empty handed to their families, they sprinkled the gold dust onto an evergreen plant they had also discovered in California. They brought this new Gold Dust Plant back east for their wives as a token of their journey. They were tired after their long journey home, and so, rested in the shade beside the Gold Dust Plant. These wives were happy to have their husbands back and a shimmering new shrub to plant in their Southern gardens.

Bambusoideae
Bamboo

Bambusoideae

Bamboo is actually in the true grass family Poaceae. Savannah is graced with a world class Bamboo research farm, The Bamboo Farm and Coastal Gardens Research Center. The Bamboo Farm, as it is known locally, is part of the University of Georgia.

Bamboo is the fastest growing woody plant on the planet. Bamboo has been used for centuries in Asian countries and around the world. Its uses range from food to scaffolding.

In ancient China artists carved it into art pieces or made furniture from it. Bamboo has been made into pipes for smoking and straws for drinking. One story even suggests that the ancient Romans used Bamboo for their aqueduct system. A modern use for Bamboo is as a renewable source for construction material.

There are many myths and legends surrounding Bamboo. One such legend, from Asia, says that humanity sprang forth from a Bamboo shoot.

As the primary food source for the lovable Panda bear, worldwide depletion of Bamboo habitats is one of the main reason for the shrinking number of Panda bears.

Planters and trees in City Market

Bougainvillea
Bougainvillea

This wonderful flowering shrub/vine gives Savannah some of its best tropical looking summer color. Bougainvillea falls down over garden walls and peeks out through wrought iron fences in a rainbow of colors, everything from orange, red and white to the brightest of fuchsias. Bougainvillea is closely related to another garden favorite, Four O'clock!

Native to South America, Bougainvillea's magical qualities have not been lost on authors and songwriters who have written much about its vibrant colors and wicked thorns. These songwriters and authors have created lyrics and prose using the tropical Bougainvillea as metaphor and inspiration for years.

So beautiful is the Bougainvillea flower, that it has inspired governments to adopt it as their official flower symbol. Independent nations such as the island of Grenada and the U.S. territory of Guam have adopted it, as well as the cities of Camarillo, Laguna Niguel and San Clemente in California.

Bougainvillea

Buddleja
Butterfly Shrub or Summer Lilac

Buddleia, as it is arguably spelled, is an all around garden favorite. Its woody stems reach six to eight feet, and most of the Summer Lilacs are evergreen in Savannah. Because Butterfly Shrub is widely planted, it would be known to most American gardeners. This old fashioned flowering shrub can be seen growing almost as far north as Chicago.

A long time ago when the forests and gardens were bare of color, the pale grey butterflies were bored and wanted something to do. The butterflies had no flowers on which to play, and they were sad.

Buddleja Davidii

Finally they decided to ask Mother Nature for help. Mother Nature, a kind woman, told the butterflies that she would create a shrub of many colors just for them. In return they were to provide as much joy to the world as the Butterfly Shrub gave to them. As the Butterfly Shrub blossomed into a fantastically colored shrub, so did the pale grey butterflies become the brilliant colors that are enjoyed today. This is why there are both the beautiful Butterfly Shrub and the motley colored butterflies that adorn it's summer flowers.

Wild Fern

Butia Capitata and *Vitis Rotundifolia*
Pindo Palm or Jelly Palm and Scuppernong

Jim Williams, a renowned architectural preservationist, restored many of the homes in Savannah's Historic District. While best known for restoring houses, he was also a garden preservationist who appreciated the restoration of a home's garden along with the home itself. Mr. Williams restored and lived in the Mercer Williams House on Monterey Square. The Mercer Williams House and Garden operates today as a house museum that is open to the public.

Mr. Williams was interested in native plants that grew well in the Southern climate. Two of the plants that he selected for the Mercer Williams House garden were the Pindo Palm and the Scuppernong Grape vine. The Pindo to the right of the front entrance, one of the most famous palms in Savannah, has graceful arching fronds that shimmer with a blue green color. This palm stands out magnificently against the Philadelphia Red Brick. The Scuppernong Grapes sprawl out across the back porch and garden walls around the carriage house. The Scuppernongs had long been a Williams' family favorite for the delicious summer grapes that were eaten fresh off the vine. The Scuppernong Grape vine gets its common name from the Scuppernong River in North Carolina. The Jelly Palm, as the name suggests, produces a fruit that Southerners have enjoyed for years.

Traditionally, both the Jelly Palm and the Scuppernong Grapes were made into jams and jellies. These preserves are still available today, along with fresh Scuppernong Grapes, at many roadside fruit stands throughout the South.

Butia photographed
by Bob Calabrese

Caesalpinia Mexicana
Mexican Bird of Paradise

Mexican Bird of Paradise is a small tree native to Texas and Mexico with bright yellow fragrant flowers from spring to fall. The foliage is finely textured and looks similar to Mimosa. Mexican Bird of Paradise may die back in the winter but it will quickly recover in the spring. This flowering tree is heat and drought tolerant and can grow to twenty feet tall. Although native to drier areas of North America, Mexican Bird of Paradise grows well in the hot and humid Savannah climate. Caesalpinia attracts bees and butterflies with brilliant colored flowers that light up as they reach for the summer sun.

Caesalpinia
Mexicana

Caladium
Heart of Jesus or Angel Wings

Today 98% of all Caladiums come from Lake Placid, Florida. Lake Placid is known world wide as the Caladium capitol of the world. Originally, Caladiums were native to Brazil, South America. Angel Wings do not flower per se, but are grown for their large colorful leaves that stand out in any semi shade garden.

Caladium

Callistemon
Bottlebrush

This Myrtle relative is a large shrub or small tree grown in Savannah for its distinctive red blossoms that emerge in late spring. It gets the common name Bottlebrush because the flower set looks like an old fashioned brush that was long and narrow, used to clean out the inside of a bottle. Bottlebrushes can come in either an upright or weeping form, and in time they develop a very rough fissured bark that is itself an outstanding attribute.

Callistemon

Cannaceae
Canna

The Canna is native to Savannah and the surrounding area. According to a legend from right here in Savannah, Cannas many colors represented the hope of the Georgia colony. Several nationalities helped to settle the fledgling colony in 1733. It was with hope and determination that these groups set aside their differences and joined in the work that was necessary for the survival of Savannah. Each group brought its own unique skills and culture to Savannah, giving the coastal colony the character it has today.

The Canna, like those settlers, comes in many varieties, each representing itself as well as the whole Canna family. The name Canna comes from the Celtic word for cane.

Canna

Cephalotaxus
Plum Yew or Podocarpus

Cephalotaxus is a large evergreen shrub or small tree reaching up to three stories if left unpruned. Plum Yew has large flat needle like leaves that resemble what a Northerner might call simply a Yew or Taxus.

There is evidence that Yew weapons have been important to Europeans for thousands of years. The oldest wooden artifact ever discovered was a Yew spear found at Clacton, England. This spear is believed to have been in use over 250,000 years ago.

One British folklore story suggests that the Yew was an understory plant, growing alongside the White Oak in groves that spread out across England. It was here under an Oak and beside the Yews in Sherwood Forest where Robin Hood met his band of Merry Men. The legend says that Robin Hood made his bow out of a Yew branch because it had magical powers of strength and accuracy. Yew branches continued to be significant in British weaponry, thus it is likely that early Savannah colonists brought the Yew from England to the New World for use in bow and spear making.

Cephalotaxus

Cercis Ssp.
Redbud or Judas Tree

In early spring the Cercis tree is covered with many pink to fuchsia colored flowers, which emerge a week or two before the leaves. The flowers have a pleasing, acrid taste and can be added to salads or mixed greens. Cercis is featured in many early herbal remedies and folklore stories from Europe.

Redbud, as it is known in North America, is a widely planted tree that would be familiar to almost all American gardeners. Redbud is a medium sized tree with irregular branches and heart shaped leaves that come in either green or burgundy.

The Judas Tree, as it is called in Christian lore, is said to be the tree from which Judas Iscariot hung himself after betraying Jesus Christ. The name may also come from "Judea's Tree" after the region to which it is native Israel, Palestine and Jordan. Cercis is also common in southern Europe, southwest Asia and into Asia Minor.

Cercis as seen in Colonial Cemetary

Chamaerops Humilis
European Fan Palm, Mediterranean Fan Palm or Camel Palm

Mediterranean Fan Palm is native to southern Europe and most of the area around the western Mediterranean. This tough, hardy Palm is a must have for any Savannah or Southeastern gardener. Its attributes are numerous and it is indispensable in the Southern landscape. European Fan Palm is easily able to withstand temperatures well below freezing for short periods of time. When other more tender palms are injured by a freeze, European Fan Palms show no sign of damage. It also withstands long periods of drought leading to the common name Camel Palm.

Mediterranean Fan Palm has wickedly anti social thorns that add to its beauty, but make placement away from play areas a necessity. This fast growing, short shrub palm often comes with multiple trunks and makes a beautiful specimen in the sometimes brutal Savannah sun.

Chamaerops Humilis

Chrysanthemum
Mum

Chrysanthemums are the symbol of many cities, including Chicago and Ju-xian in China. Mums are also the symbol of several Japanese emperors as well as a number of organizations.

Mums are, for most of us here in America, a symbol of autumn. The Mum is a fall flowering annual or perennial that tells us of shorter days and cooler weather. Mums, Pumpkins and dried corn stalks are often featured together with witches and ghosts in autumn yard displays.

Chrysanthemum

Citrus Poncirus Trifoliata x
Citrus Sinensis x Fortunella
Thomasville Citrangequat

'Thomasville' is a sibling of 'Telfair' that first fruited in Thomasville, Georgia. In a botanical name sequence, an x between names means that it is a hybrid of those plants. 'Thomasville's' fruit is a little larger than the other two citrangequats and it is somewhat seedy. 'Thomasville' is considered edible at full maturity. Most people think of citrus fruit growing only in Florida, however several kinds of citrus do well in the Savannah landscape.

Citrus

Clematis
Clematis or Traveler's Joy

The large showy flowers of Clematis are often grown in window boxes and in the gardens of Savannah. Clematis can be seen growing on gates, fences and stair rails throughout the Historic District. Clematis is named Traveler's Joy because it peeks out around corners and over hedgerows and says "Hi, Welcome to Savannah!" to the many visitors that travel here from around the world. No matter where you live, when you get back home and see a Clematis flower, be sure to remember Savannah and the warm welcome of Traveler's Joy.

Clematis

Crassula Ovata
Jade or Friendship Plant

A popular house or Bonsai plant, that can be grown outside, year-round in Savannah, needing only a shady spot. A gardener needs to water a Jade Plant sparingly, as it is a succulent. Jade grows quickly under the right conditions, in time growing to be well over three feet tall.

Crassula Ovata

Crinum
Crinum Lily

Crinum Lilies are an outstanding flowering perennial in the Savannah garden. They are a member of the Amaryllidaceae family, making them related to the Amaryllis. Although they are often called a Lily, Crinums are only very distantly related to lilies. Crinums are more accurately called an herb, with many medicinal uses. Crinums are native to Africa, but grow in subtropical regions all over the world.

In Christian symbolism, the pure white flower of the Crinum Lily has represented purity and delicateness for many years.

Crinum as seen in the author's garden

Codiaeum
Croton or Milon of Croton

Codiaeum is a Euphorbia in the family Euphorbiaceae. They are native to the South Pacific. They are often shrubs with large motley colored leaves

and often confused with the genus Croton. Croton is simply a common name. Croton gets its name from Milo or Milon of Croton, the most famous athlete in Greek mythology.

Milo emerged in a glorious flash of color from the Croton shrub in the sixth century BCE. He was destined to be an Olympic champion from birth and so because of the Croton, the Olympic colors were first used by Milo to signal the strength and discipline of the athlete.

Croton

He was, in all likelihood, a historical person, as he is mentioned by many Greek writers in the years following his life. He is, in other writings, given credit for commanding the Crotonian army that defeated the Sybarites in about 500 BCE, while wearing his Olympic Crown of Croton leaves. It is quite a colorful shrub that compliments Milo's colorful life.

Cryptomeria
Sugi or Japanese Cryptomeria

Sugi is the national tree of Japan, commonly planted around temples and shrines, with many very impressive trees planted centuries ago. History tells the story of a Japanese feudal lord who was too poor to give the traditional stone lantern at the funeral of the Emperor of Nikko Tosho Gu. Instead he requested to be allowed to plant an avenue of Sugi so that future visitors might be protected from the heat of the sun. The request was accepted, and the avenue leading to the Emperor's crypt was planted. The avenue of Cryptomerias, which still lives today, is over forty miles long and has yet to be equaled in stately grandeur.

Cryptomeria trees are extensively planted in gardens and parks in Japan and China and are also widely grown as an ornamental tree in other warm climate areas, including Europe and America.

Cryptomeria

Orchid arrangement

Cunninghamia Lanceolata
Cunninghamia or Chinese Fir

This towering evergreen is native to China and Vietnam. The botanical name Lanceolata comes from an old Chinese military story.

Centuries ago, China was a poor country struggling to survive. Through the years many emperors had been defeated by invading armies. Out numbered and under equipped, the Chinese army was doomed to failure yet again until the mighty Cunninghamia Lanceolata volunteered to be a soldier. Because its deep roots made the Cunninghamia immobile, it offered to the service of China the only thing it had, its lance shaped needles. Newly armed with thousands of lances, the Chinese army could now take on any invaders that dared to challenge it. The Chinese emperor, grateful for its contribution, granted the Chinese Fir its enormous size so that it could stand proudly above the other soldiers and lead the Chinese army into victorious battle.

Cunninghamia

Curcuma
Ginger

Two types of Ginger can be found in Savannah gardens. The first type is a large leafed, often variegated, tropical looking foliage plant. The second type is much smaller and is grown for its soft pinkish white or reddish white flowers. While both these plants are related to the culinary Ginger, they are grown by Savannah gardeners' as ornamentals.

Curcuma

Cycad
Dioon or Giant Sago Palm

Dioon was known for centuries as "The Savannah Monster." Long before massive Oaks or mighty Ginkgos ruled the forest floor, ferns were king. Sprawling out over the world, ferns had emerged from the muck and provided the lizards and dragonflies with shade and shelter. Then, along came the Dioon rising from the depths of the earth. Much like a fern, the Dioon unfurled its mighty fronds. Alas, the Dioon was not a fern. It developed a stout thick trunk as it pushed up over the confused and frightened ferns. The Dioon's enormous fronds seemed to reach out forever to the earthly ferns who stared up in wonder at this tree above them. Soon though, the Dioon provided the ferns with much needed shade from the blazing summer sun, and the ferns realized that the Dioon was not some beast to be feared, but rather a kind friend who provided rest under its fan of fronds.

Cycad Dioon

Cyperus Papyrus
Papyrus Plant or Sedge

Papyrus is a Sedge plant in the Grass family. It is native to Africa and was traditionally grown along the banks of the Nile. Historically, Papyrus was harvested, dried and used to make paper. The first paper was originally made out of Papyrus. Papyrus was also a food source for early Egyptians.

Papyrus can be found growing in all parts of Savannah, giving the gardens an interesting and historical feel. While Papyrus is a valuable ornamental plant, its cousin, Sedge Weed, is an invasive nuisance to Savannah gardeners.

Papyrus is tall with a distinctive leaf pattern, a whirl at the top of a long cylindrical spike. Sedge weed has a similar leaf pattern, but is short with a triangular stem, a separate identification feature.

Cyperus Papyrus

Cyrtomium Falcatum
Japanese Holly Fern

The Chinese Emperor Qinzong, of the Song Dynasty, wanted to invade Japan. The year was 1127 when Emperor Qinzong devised a plan to infiltrate Japan. The Emperor secretly put his soldiers into the spores on the back of the Holly Fern fronds and introduced the fern to Japan. The Japanese thought the Holly Fern was a beautiful gift from their neighboring country. The Japanese planted the fern all over Japan. When the time came for the invasion, Emperor Qinzong ordered his soldiers to emerge and they did. The Chinese soldiers looked around them and said "Look at this beautiful country! We can't possibly invade here." So, they planted themselves and became part of the natural beauty of Japan, thereby foiling Emperor Qinzong's invasion of Japan. This is how the Holly Fern became the Japanese Holly Fern.

Cyrtomium Falcatum

Daubentonia
Punicea or Sesbania Punicea
Rattlebox or Rattlebox Tree

Although native to South America, Daubentonia Punicea grows well in all tropical or sub-tropical climates throughout the Americas, including the Savannah landscape.

Chooktul, the protector of children in an ancient Mayan legend from the Yucatan peninsula, tells us the tale of the Rattlebox. Chooktul knew and loved all of the Mayan children and enjoyed watching them play and grow. He knew, also, that it was a dangerous world and that rattlesnakes lived in the shrubs and flowers in which the Mayan children played. Chooktul kept a close eye on the rattlesnakes and when one came too close to the children, he turned the children into the rattlebox tree. The children would then shake their seed pods like a rattle. The snake, fearing that a much larger snake was near, would slither away. The boys and girls would then be safe from the venomous bite of the rattlesnake. The youngsters were unaware of the danger as Chooktul changed the Rattlebox Tree back into the children.

Daubentonia

Delosperma Cooperi
Ice Plant or African Ice Plant

Ice Plant is a succulent perennial with the most brilliant fuchsia flower color in the Savannah garden. This wonderful groundcover blooms all summer. African Ice Plant, possibly named for its crystal, frosty appearance, is native to South Africa. A new cultivar that has a sandy yellow colored flower has also recently become available.

Delospermum

Dietes
African Iris

Native to Southern Africa. The African Iris has a tri-petaled flower resembling the woodland perennial Trillium.

Dietes

Duranta Erecta
Golden Dewdrop

Duranta is a truly tropical flowering shrub that grows well in the deep south, but it's size in Savannah is smaller than in its native range.

Duranta Erecta

This irregular shrub is native to South and Central America. The deep purple flower of the Duranta is among the most royal of the flower colors available in the Savannah landscape. Duranta gets its common name because the small fruit it produces resembles a golden dewdrop.

Ericaceae
Heath or Heather

Heather is as much a symbol of Scotland as the famous Thistle, especially in the Highlands where it grows in abundance. The Picts, a nomadic Scottish tribe, were recognized for their Heath ale. This drink has been made for many centuries in the Scottish Highlands. The Picts were said to make this fine ale solely from Heath, no Hops or Malt were added. The Heath ales fermentation process relied exclusively on the Heath blooms and nectar for the flavor.

A legend tells how in the fifth century the Norse defeated a Pictish army, slaying everyone but their king and his son. The Norse cornered them on a cliff. The victorious Norse hoped to extract the secret recipe for the Heath ale from the king and his son. After being tortured, the Pictish king offered to reveal the recipe, but only if his son died a painless death. The young prince was quickly thrown over the cliff, after which the Pictish king revealed that though he would be able to keep the recipe a secret, he had had doubts as to his son's ability to keep the secret. With that, he tussled with the Norse chief and flung them both over the cliff taking the Heath ale recipe with him to his grave.

Ericaceae
Heath

Eriobotrya Japonica
Loquat

A medium size, evergreen fruit tree. Loquats produce a wonderful, small fruit that tastes like a cross between an apricot and a mango. Loquat fruit matures in February and March here in Savannah. The fruit can be eaten straight off the tree, but should be consumed in moderation. This Japanese native should be considered for any Japanese style peace garden.

Eriobotrya Japonica

Erythrina
Coral Bean

Coral Bean has been adopted by many American Christians as a symbol of their faith. Coral Bean has a trifoliate leaf that is said to illustrate the Trinity, as well as bright red flowers that represent the blood of Christ. Coral Bean also produces a bean that demonstrates the abundance of the harvest in Christian teachings. Because of its religious symbolism, this plant is often seen as a cemetery planting. There are numerous specimens of *Erythrina* at historic Bonaventure Cemetery in Savannah.

The *Erythrina* species most commonly found here in Savannah is a small shrub that fits well into any landscape and requires little care once established. Coral Bean is deciduous with flowers that emerge in the spring before the leaves come out.

Erythrina

Eschscholzia Californica
California Poppy or Poppy

The California Poppy is a garden favorite in Savannah. This Poppy is a grassland wildflower native to the western United States, from California North to Oregon and East to New Mexico. The Poppy brings its bright yellow and orange color to the late spring landscape here in Georgia.

Because of the humidity in Savannah, the California Poppy goes down as the heat of the summer rises, but they make a return later in the autumn as temperatures fall again. The California Poppy is the California state flower.

Eschscholzia

Euphorbia
Poinsettia or Christmas Star

Poinsettias are an all time Christmas favorite for Americans. Poinsettias, native to Mexico, do well outside in the Southern climate of Savannah. While most of us are familiar with the Christmas plant with bright red leaves, which are actually bracts, there is a wild variety here in Savannah. Because of the familiarity with the Christmas Poinsettia; pictured here is a photograph of the less well known wild variety. All Poinsettias, both wild and cultivated, bract. Bracting is the changing of leaf color from green to, in this case, red or orange, giving the leaf a petal like appearance. Poinsettia flowers actually have no petals, only leaves that have bracted.

The Poinsettias association with Christmas originated in the 1500's in Mexico, where legend tells of a young senorita, who was too poor to give a gift for the celebration of Jesus' birthday. The legend goes that the girl was

inspired by an angel to gather weeds from the roadside and place them on the altar of her local church. Bright red "blossoms" sprouted from the weeds and became beautiful poinsettias.

Euphorbia

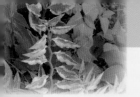

Euphorbia or Pedilanthus
Devil's Backbone

Pedilanthus is a succulent Spurge. It grows in the wild and is native to both North and Central America. It is also kept as a houseplant. The bracts of Euphorbia are pinkish to red in color. It has unique zigzag stems, and comes in both green and variegated forms.

In Bolivia, it is often steeped into a psychedelic brew, along with mescaline. This brew brings about wild and bizarre imaginary visions, when consumed next to a fire in the dark of the night, including sightings of the devil. According to accounts, many drinking the Pedilanthus brew saw visions of the devil himself rising out of the campfire, with his crooked spine and outstretched arms, he reached for the drinkers before his hands turned into red hot Pedilanthus leaves. The devil's contorted figure kept reaching for the sky only to disappear into a cloud of smoke. When morning came, all that was left was a Devil's Backbone plant waving in the warm Bolivian sun.

Euphorbia Pedilanthus

Feijoa Sellowiana
Pineapple Guava

The Pineapple Guava is a flowering and fruiting tree native to Columbia and Uruguay in South America. Pineapple Guava is a medium sized evergreen shrub in the Savannah landscape. The bright red flowers of the Guava come out in early spring and resemble a crown, as the stamen set is on the outside of the style.

Feijoa Sellowiana

Ficus Carica
Common Fig

Ficus Carica is the botanical name for the Common Fig. The Fig is a large shrub grown in Savannah, throughout the South and around the world for its large plump fruit that can be eaten fresh off the shrub.

Historically, the Fig has played a consistent part in cultures around the world. Fig wood was used by early Egyptians to make mummy cases, as better wood was scarce in such a treeless land. The fruit of the Fig was, and is, a staple in the diets of many peoples around the Mediterranean Sea, its native area.

One story from the region tells of Calchas, who, when challenged by his fellow prophet, Mopsus, to a contest of soothsaying, was unable to throw back the gauntlet. In the legend Mopsus said, "Yonder Fig tree has 9999 fruit", a count that proved correct. Calchas was unable to guess anything of more importance, and hated himself to death under the branches of the Fig. The 9999 fruits came to represent his tears.

Ficus Carica

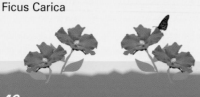

Ficus Pumila
Creeping Fig

An old fashioned Southern plant, Creeping Fig has historically been, planted and maintained on many of the seventeen and eighteenth century homes in Savannah's Historic District. When classically pruned, Creeping Fig will be sheared flat against a wall or house and trimmed tight to the door and window frames. It will also be pruned to a height of about one third the height of the home it is being trained on. Because of the constant shearing that Creeping Fig takes to maintain, its fruit set is often sacrificed. When Creeping Fig is left to grow untrimmed, it will develop a much larger and leathery leaf that arches out from whatever building it is growing on. Creeping Fig is a true fig and, left uncut, it will produce medium sized figs that must be pollinated by a fig wasp. Creeping Figs are not as sweet as store bought figs, but are edible none the less. Creeping Fig is also related to the Mulberry tree, another important and historical plant here in Savannah.

Ficus Pumila

Ficus Pumila

Gaillardia
Gaillardia, Firewheel or Blanket Flower

Gaillardia is a reliable perennial in the Savannah border. This Aster wildflower is native to dry, sunny terrains across North America.

Blanket Flower derives its common name from Native American blanket patterns that were inspired by the blanket of Gaillardia flowers that covered the plains in brilliant reds and oranges. Many Native American tribes would have been familiar with Gaillardia and incorporated its sun pattern into art motifs.

While Native Americans did not worship the sun in the same way that ancient Egyptians did, they certainly acknowledged its power and were inspired by it. Native Americans also saw in the Gaillardia the powerful image of the sun, and painted it on shields, horses and homes for inspiration and protection. In this context, it was referred to as Firewheel.

Gaillardia

Savannah Street Garden

Gardenia
Gardenia

The Gardenia is a classic old fashioned landscape shrub in the South. What is most often recognized about the Gardenia is the pure white flower that is widely known for its scent. Described as both sweet and heavy, the scent of the Gardenia flower is unmistakable in the late spring and early summer. Gardenias can be fussy, but generally grows well in shady places that are fairly humid. The Gardenia is a medium to large evergreen.

The Gardenia was named by Carlos Linnaeus in the 1700s for his friend, Dr. Alexander Garden, a Scottish botanist and physician.

Gardenia

Ginkgo Biloba
The Dinosaur Tree

In August of 1945 the United States bombed Hiroshima, Japan. In September of 1945 the United States went back to do a survey and found a completely decimated city, with the exception of four Ginkgo Biloba trees. Each of these trees was over 200 years old, and all four of these trees were alive and well.

Ginkgo

In Japan, there is an indigenous religion called Shinto. Shintoism is not a deity based religion; however it does have a supreme spirit that is called Kami. The Shinto belief is that the Kami lives in the Ginkgo. The Kami protects the Ginkgo and the Ginkgo protects the Kami. This is why the Shinto belief is that the four Ginkgo trees survived the blast.

When the City of Hiroshima built back the four municipal Shinto Temples, they built them facing each of the four surviving Ginkgo trees. The stairwells were built around the trunks of the trees leading into the temples. The stairwells were built this way because in Shintoism the belief is when one enters the temple one brings Kami in with them and when one exits, they leave Kami in the Ginkgo tree for the next worshipper.

The Dinosaur Tree is native to Japan, China and Korea. It is called the Dinosaur Tree because of its ancient fossil record.

Ginkgo Biloba provides Savannah with some of its best fall color when the leaves turn a brilliant yellow in mid-November.

Gloriosa Rothschildiana
Gloriosa Lily or Flame Lily

Ever since the Gloriosa Lily was featured on a U.S. postage stamp, at the thirty-three-cent rate, it has been sought out by Southern gardeners looking to add its exotic and unusual flower to their gardens. Gloriosa Lily makes an outstanding cut flower in arrangements but is rarely seen in floral shops.

Flower arrangers who want this colorful flower will probably need to grow it themselves. The configuration of its stamens and pistil has been compared to the Martigon Lily and to the eternal flame, where it gets its most widely used common name. Flame Lily is the national flower of Zimbabwe, Africa. Gloriosa Lilies are a climbing or sprawling member of the Lilium family and are native to South Africa. In the Gloriosa photograph on the cover, a Stokesia Cyanea (Stokes Aster) with a warm lavender flower can be seen in the background.

Gloriosa

Hedera Canariensis
Algerian Ivy

Despite it's common name Algerian Ivy is not native to Algeria. It is native to the Canary Islands and related to the English Ivy as the botanical name would suggest. This is one of several African plants that will grow well in Savannah. It has been lost to history why a vine from Morocco is named Algerian anything. The Algerian Ivy pictured here is variegated, but it comes in an all green variety as well. Canary Island Date Palm (Phoenix Canariensis) is also native to the Canary Islands. The Canary Islands are off the west coast of Morocco in Northwest Africa.

Hedera Canariensis

Hedera Helex
English Ivy

Both loved and loathed by gardeners worldwide, Hedera Helex is the world's most widely grown Ivy. It is seen growing

all over America, where it is called English Ivy.

In a Greek mythological legend it was named Cissos, because according to the legend, it was named after the Greek nymph Cissos. Cissos, at a feast of the gods, danced before Dionysus with such fervor and abandon that she dropped dead from exhaustion at his feet. Dionysus was so moved by her passion and untimely death that he turned her body into the Ivy, where even today she is still seen joyfully dancing and embracing everything she sees.

Hedera Helix

Dedicated to the wine god Dionysus, she can still be seen intertwined with grape leaves in wreaths and garlands in wine shops and taverns around the world.

Helianthus
Sunflower

Over the years, various plants have been known as the Sunflower. Chrysanthemum, Dandelion, and Rudbeckia have all been called Sunflower, but it is Helianthus Annuus that is most commonly called the Sunflower by the modern gardener.

For centuries, the Sunflower has been a symbol of the sun, the most powerful of the icons worshipped by both ancient and modern earth religions. In ancient Peru, sun worshippers wore Sunflowers as a representation of the sphere they worshipped. The high priestess wore Sunflowers made of gold. The gold attracted the attention of the invading Spaniards, who branded the Sunflowers a symbol of these unauthorized religions and took the gold for themselves while putting the sun worshippers to the sword.

Helianthus

Hemerocallis
Daylily

Daylilies comprise the small genus Hemerocallis of flowering plants in the family Hemerocallidaceae. They are not true lilies, which are Lilium, but are a relative of New Zealand Flax. These plants are grown in Savannah gardens as a perennial. The name Hemerocallis comes from the Greek word Hemera, meaning day and the word kalos, meaning beautiful.

The flowers open at sunrise and close at sunset. A new flower emerges each day throughout the summer. There are now hundreds of flower colors and petal shapes to choose from, as hybridizers have created an almost endless number of varieties.

Daylilies are originally native to Europe, China and Japan. Their dependability, adaptability and bright summer flowers have made them popular around the world.

The flowers of some varieties have culinary uses and are used in Chinese cooking. They are sold fresh or dried in Chinese food stores as golden needles or yellow flower vegetables. They are used in Daylily soup, Buddha's Delight and Moo Shu pork recipes. The green leaves of some varieties are also eaten in Asian countries.

Hemerocallis

Old Man of the tree

Hibiscus
Hibiscus or Tropical Hibiscus

Hibiscus has long been a symbol of tropical areas. Several types of Hibiscus grow well in Savannah gardens, giving them a warm tropical flare. What picture of Hawaii, Florida or Cuba would be complete without including a Hibiscus? In both Hawaii and Cuba woman wear Hibiscus flowers behind the ear. Which ear they wear it on indicates whether or not they are available for marriage. Hibiscus is also the state flower of Hawaii.

Gardeners from the Mid Atlantic and Mid Western states know Hibiscus as Rose of Sharon or Althea, and this is appropriate as they are all in the Malvaceae family and all look very similar.

The Hibiscus flower is used as an offering to the goddess Kali and the deity Vinayaka during worship in the Hindu tradition.

Hibiscus

Hibiscus

Hibiscus

Hosta
Hosta

Although native to China and Japan, Hostas have become a classic shade plant in modern gardens. Many types of Hosta are available. They are known for their clumping habit and usually large leaves that can be variegated or all green, depending on the variety. Hostas need to be divided every few years and make a great gift for friends. All Hosta plants produce a tall inflorescence spike with light, almost pale purple flowers.

Hosta

Houttuynia Cordata
Chameleon Plant or Fish Mint

Chameleon Plant is a Savannah garden favorite, a Southern favorite. Grown for its lovely heart shaped leaves and unique ability to become similar to the other plants around it. Plant a Chameleon in your garden, in any moist and shady spot, and watch as it turns into or mimics in some way the plants around it. For example, in the photograph, it is next to a variegated Ginger, with stripes of yellow and green. Notice how the Chameleon Plant is turning the exact same shades of yellow and green and also variegated, as the Ginger Plant. Put with another plant, it will adopt the color scheme or other attributes of that plant. It is almost disappointing that Houttuynia tries to blend in so well, because it really is a fascinating addition to any garden.

Houttuynia is native to Vietnam, China and Korea where it is used as a leafy vegetable and fresh herbal garnish. It got its other common name, Fish Mint, because of the unusual "fishy" flavor of the leaves. It is a bit of an acquired taste and so it is not enjoyed as universally as basil, mint, or other more commonly used herbs. Although Houttuynia is a unique and acquired taste, it is well worth trying.

Houttuynia

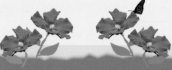

Hydrangea
Hydrangea

Hydrangea is without a doubt a garden classic. Hydrangeas have been planted for years in gardens across Europe and America. Hydrangeas are grown most often for their large flower clusters that bloom in the spring and often last until frost in late November. They should always be planted in a shady location and need plenty of water during the hot summer months.

For most types of Hydrangeas the flowers are white, but in some species the flower can be blue, pink or purple. In many varieties of Hydrangeas the exact color often depends on the PH of the soil; acidic soils produce blue flowers, neutral soils produce pale cream flowers and alkaline soils result in pink or purple. Gardeners love that they can change the flower color to suit their particular gardens. Hydrangeas are also used as a dried flower in arrangements and for arts and crafts.

Hydrangea

Hypoestes Phyllostachya
Splash

Splash is a fun, colorful, tropical plant and a regular in Savannah gardens. Splash is a perennial in the South, but is grown as an annual in the North. This small plant gets its common name from the Splash of color it brings to any summertime garden.

Hypoestes Phyllostachya

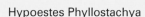

Ilex Cornuta Rotunda
Christmas Holly or Chinese Horned Holly

According to a Christian legend, the Holly mysteriously grew leaves in the midsts of winter to hide baby Jesus and his parents from Herod's soldiers. Since then, the Holly tree has been an evergreen as a token of Christ's gratitude.

Another legend about this Christmas plant says that a little boy was living with the shepherds when the angels came to announce the birth of Jesus. Having no gift for the baby, the young boy wove a crown of Holly branches for the Christ child's head. But when the crown was laid before the baby Jesus, the little shepherd became ashamed of the crown's poverty and began to cry. Jesus touched the crown and miraculously it turned to gold; meanwhile, the shepherd boy's tears became the bright red berries.

In Bavaria, the Holly is called Christdorn referring to Christ's crown of thorns. According to a legend, during the crucifixion, the Holly leaves were woven into a painful crown and placed on Christ's head while the Roman soldiers mocked him. The Holly berries were white but Christ's blood left them a permanent crimson red.

Many superstitions surround the Holly in England. It is believed to be a man's plant and is thought to bring good luck and protection to men, while Ivy brings the same good fortune to women. It is said that whoever brings

the first sprig of Christmas Holly into the home will lead the family that year. Garlands of Holly were hung about the house to keep away witches, goblins, spells, evil spirits and lightning. However, elves and fairies were welcome in British households and sprigs of Holly were hung as places for them to hide.

Ancient Romans gave Holly boughs as gifts to their friends and lovers, as good luck charms, during the unrestrained revelry of the Saturnalian festival that was celebrated in December.

Because of these pagan superstitions, early Christians were forbidden to decorate with this plant. Eventually these superstitions were laid to rest and the Holly has become a symbol for Christians of this most cherished holiday. It has also become a classic American landscape shrub, seen in yards across this country as well as in Europe.

Ilex Cornuta Rotundafolia

Ilex x Attenuata
Savannah Holly

Welcome to Savannah! The Savannah Holly welcomes visitors to our fair city year round with large bright green leaves, deep red berries and a tall pyramid shape that is both commanding and graceful. Although native to China botanically, it was growing here when the first Georgia colonists arrived in 1733 and has been a staple of the Savannah landscape for almost three hundred years.

Ilex x Attenuata

Garden at The Green-Meldrim House

Iris
Iris

Iris is a perennial with showy flowers which takes its name from the Greek word for rainbow, referring to the wide variety of flower colors found among the many species. Iris was the flower of the Royal House of France, depicted as the well known symbol, the Fleur-de-lis.

"The Rainbow Goddess Collection" is an award winning Iris display housed in Savannah at the Bamboo Farm and Coastal Gardens. This collection of more than 400 varieties of Tall Bearded Iris is owned and maintained by Stan Gray.

Anvil of Darkness

Knock 'em Dead

Arctic Fox

Fatal Attraction

Lovely Senorita

Social Graces

Swingtown

Juniperus Chinensis 'Torulosa'
Torture Juniper or Hollywood Juniper

Carolus Linnaeus is the Swiss botanist who is widely credited with developing the modern Binomial system of botanical nomenclature, or double scientific name system. He is also the father of Biological Taxonomy.

It was Carolus Linnaeus who named the Juniperus Chinensis 'Torulosa' after the Latin word for torture. He thought the branch structure looked like "People being tortured in the flames of Hell," referring to the old European museum paintings of such contorted subjects. With its twisted branches flung to the sky, it is easy to imagine the Juniper 'Torulosa' looking like a flame as well.

Juniperus Chinensis 'Torulosa'

Justicia
Shrimp Plant

Shrimp Plant is one of several truly tropical plants that flourish here. Savannah is as far north as the Justicia plant can be grown. The common name Shrimp Plant comes from the shape of the flower that looks like the body of a shrimp.

Justicia

Kalanchoe
Mother-of-Millions or Alien Cactus

Kalanchoe is an alien looking succulent that grows little offsets of itself on the margin of its leaves. Mother-of-Millions can look very uniform or quite varied in its leaf structure, leading to the common name Alien Cactus. Mother-of-Millions is not really a cactus because it can live in any regular garden soil. A gardener must be careful with Alien Cactus because once it is established in the garden it is likely to be there forever. Mother-of-Millions comes in several flower colors, including red, yellow or white.

Kalanchoe

Lagerstroemia Indica
Crape Myrtle

Crape Myrtle is widely known throughout the United States as "the Lilac of the South." This tree gives the South both its best summer flower color and its best fall color. Crape Myrtle's easy care and wide range of colors and sizes make it a garden and landscape favorite. The bark and branch structure are two of the Lagerstroemias best attributes.

Lagerstroemia Indica – branch structure

Lagerstroemia Indica

The bark patterns and the branch structure are often overlooked, but can be appreciated in the winter when there are no leaves.

Crape Myrtles should never be cut back wholesale, that is, by a third or by half. This bad pruning practice is called pollarding, and while it creates more flowers in the short term, in the long term it mangles and kills the tree. Landscapers call pollarding "Crape murder". A Crape Myrtle should only be lightly pruned; just enough to cut out die back and suckers.

Lagerstroemia Indica

Lagerstroemia Indica

Lagerstroemia Indica

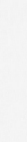

Lagerstroemia Indica

Lagerstroemia Indica

Lagerstroemia
Indica - bark

Lantana Camara
Lantana

One species native to South America, Lantana Camara, has been introduced horticulturally throughout much of the world, and now it is planted in many Savannah gardens to attract butterflies. The Savannah gardener has many colors from which to choose when they put Lantana in the landscape.

Lantana is becoming known as a metaphor for our lives as it gains popularity as a garden shrub. Neat but textured leaves of a pleasing matte green form the background for a stunning and beautiful flower. In the height of its flowering period, Lantana shrubs are covered with a brilliant, rich kaleidoscope of color. Lantana appears in many ways the way we would like to be seen. However, the inside of a Lantana shrub under the pretty exterior is often a tangled and complicated mess of branches. So it is in its totality, a lot like us, beautiful and attractive on the outside and a bit more ensnarled on the inside.

Lantana Camara

Savannah Garden

Lilium Asiaticum
Lily

This is the classic Mother's Day lily. Lilies come in several colors: white, pink, yellow, and red, as pictured.

Lilium Asiaticum

Liriope
Monkey Grass or Lilly Turf

Monkey grass is a common border plant. Liriope is, in Savannah, an evergreen plant that produces a purple flower inflorescence in the late summer.

Liriope is the mother of Narcissus in Greek Mythology.

Liriope

Livistona Decipiens
Ribbon Fan Palm

A slender, tall palm with graceful arching fronds, Ribbon Fan Palm is rare in Savannah. However, it is worthy of inclusion in the Savannah landscape. Ribbon Palm is one of the most stunning and beautiful palms that can be seen growing here in the coastal South. It has long ribbon like lobes, or sections, on each frond leading to the common name Ribbon Palm. This palm is native to Queensland, Australia.

Livistona Decipiens

Lonicera
Honeysuckle or Woodbine

Honeysuckle has long been a garden favorite in Savannah, as well as the rest of America. Honeysuckle gets its common name from the flowers that appear in the spring and continue into the summer. Many Americans can remember, as children, pulling out the flower stamen and getting a drop of sweet honey. Honeysuckle tasting is a wonderful treat not to be missed.

Woodbine, as it is also called, has a unique leaf structure unseen on other vines. The first few leaves along the stem encircle the stem completely, creating an unusual leaf arrangement. This leaf structure gives Woodbine its texture and overall shape. As a vine, it flows over garden gates and fences in a special way that makes it an American garden classic.

Lonicera Honeysuckle

Loropetalum
Fringe Flower or Witch Hazel

A Christian folk legend tells an alternate story of Adam and Eve after the garden of Eden.

When Adam was expelled from paradise, God pitied him so much that he allowed him to create new animals by striking water with a Hazel rod. Adam, after having produced a sheep, incurred the wrath of a jealous Eve. With the Hazel rod and a steady hand she brought a wolf into the world, which forthwith sprang at the sheep. Adam regained the Hazel branch and struck the water, and with that, summoned into existence a dog that overpowered the wolf.

Loropetalum

This Christian legend, in turn, brought about the old European story of the Hazel branch being used as a divining rod, with which a source of underground water might be found. With the help of a divining rod, Old World farmers would know where to dig for a well.

Along with many other plants, Loropetalum can be seen on the Greenfeet Walkabouts botanical tour of Savannah.

Morus
Mulberry

In 1733, the British were competing with a large and robust silk industry in France. So, England dreamed of silk textiles as well. This was the main reason the Georgia colonists started The Trustees' Garden, not as a culinary garden, but as a commercial garden.

Silkworms produce silk and are necessary to the silk industry. No silkworms, no silk. Mulberry trees are also necessary to the production of silk, as they are the main food source for silkworms. Mulberry trees were brought up from the British West Indies to Savannah for the sole purpose of feeding the silkworms. The Mulberry trees did fine in the harsh Georgia climate, but the silkworms themselves did not. In Savannah, it was too cold for tropical silkworms and too hot for Northern silkworms. After several years of trying to produce silk, only eight pounds were ever manufactured.

Morus

The many Mulberry trees that can be seen around Savannah today are descendents of the original colonial Mulberry trees, while the many other original plants including Flax that were grown in The Trustees' Garden have disappeared. The Trustees' Garden itself no longer exists, but was located near the site of The Pirate's House restaurant on East Broad St.

The Author's Garden

Musa
Banana

Musa is the botanical name for one of the world's most common foods, the banana. Musa is Arabic for Moses.

Technically an herb, Musa is a most unusual plant because it produces a fruit. Typically, herbs do not produce fruit. The yellow fruit set seen in the photograph are young, developing bananas.

Musa

Myrica Cerifera
Wax Myrtle or Bayberry

A Roman mythological legend tells the story of Myricus, the rogue son of Mercury. In his human form it was Myricus who took a bribe from Pelopilius to pull a pin from his master's chariot wheel. This enabled Pelopilius to win a race against Myricus's master and thereby claim the master's daughter as his bride. In return, the master showed little appreciation, for he seized Myricus and flung him out to sea, scorning the traitor he had become. Alas, the sea would not have him either, and tossed him back ashore. As punishment for betraying his master in pursuit of love, his human form was taken from him and he became the Myrica Tree.

Myrica Cerifera

Wax Myrtle gets one of its common names from the fact that the early colonists here in Savannah used its waxy berries to make candles. Myrica also has properties that ward off mosquitoes.

Myrtus Communis
Common Myrtle

In Jewish tradition, there is a fall harvest festival named Sukkot, or Feast of the Tabernacles. An observance during Sukkot involves plants that are known as the Four Species. The four species are a Myrtle, a Willow, a Date Palm and a Citrus fruit known as an Etrog. The branches of these species, along with the Etrog, are bound together and referred to collectively as the Lulav. Jews are commanded to take these four plants and use them to "Rejoice before the Lord". While holding branches of three of the species and the Etrog fruit, one recites a blessing and waves the four species in all six directions (North, South, East, West, Up and Down), symbolizing the fact that God is everywhere. The four species are also held and waved during the Hallel prayer in religious services and are held during processions, called Hakafot, around the Bimah each day during the holiday.

In one version of the Sukkot tradition, the long straight Date Palm branch represents the spine. The small oval Myrtle Leaf represents the eye. The long oval Willow Leaf represents the mouth. The Etrog, a citrus native to Israel, represents the heart. All of these parts have the potential to be used for sin, but should instead be joined together in the performance of the commandments, called mitzvot.

Myrtus

In another version, the Etrog, which has both a pleasing taste and scent, represents Jews who have achieved both knowledge of Torah and performance of mitzvot. The Palm Branch, which produces tasty fruit, but has no scent, represents Jews who have knowledge of Torah but are lacking in mitzvot. The Myrtle Leaf, which has a strong scent but no taste, represents Jews who perform mitzvot but have little knowledge of Torah. The Willow, which has neither taste nor scent, represents Jews who have no knowledge of Torah and do not perform the mitzvot. Jews bring all four of these species together on Sukkot to remind them that every one of these four kinds of Jews is important, and that Jews must all be united.

This specimen may be seen in the garden at the Juliette Gordon Low Birthplace House museum.

Nelumbo Nucifera
Lotus, Bean of India or Sacred Lotus

Nelumbo is a variety of aquatic plant with large, showy flowers that are similar to Water Lilies, commonly called Lotus or Sacred Lotus. The botanical name is derived from the Sinhalese word Nelum. The Lotus Flower or Bean of India, as it is sometimes called, has become the National Flower of India. The Lotus plant has many traditional culinary uses.

From ancient times the Lotus has been a divine symbol for Hindus. In India, Hindu mythology associates the Lotus blossom with the gods Vishnu and Brahma, as well as with the goddesses Sarasvati and Lakshmi. Often used as an example of divine beauty, Vishnu is traditionally described as the 'Lotus-Eyed One'. Mythology of the Lotus tells the story of the expansion of the soul through the unfolding of the petals. The growth of this beautiful flower, from its origin of muck, holds a magnificent spiritual promise. In Hindu iconography, gods are often depicted sitting or standing on Lotus flowers. In the Hindi language the Lotus is named Kamal which is also a popular name for men. For example, Georg Joseph Kamel, a well known botanist, had the Camellia named for him by Carlos Linnaeus. Linnaeus named the Camellia for Kamel because Linnaeus realized that the Lotus flower and the Camellia flower looked similar.

In Buddhist tradition, the Lotus plant represents purity of body and mind. It imagines the soul suspended above the filthy waters of attachment and desire. The Buddha is often shown sitting on a giant Lotus leaf or blossom. According to legend, he was born with the ability to walk on Lotus leaves that were floating on the surface of the water. On every leaf on which he stepped, a Lotus flower emerged in splendor.

Inspired by Hindu and Buddhist beliefs, the Bahá'í faith used the symbolism of the opening of the Lotus flower in the design of its house of worship, referred to as the Lotus Temple, in the city of New Delhi, India.

Nelumbo at Bamboo Farm & Coastal Gardens

Nelumbo at Bamboo Farm & Coastal Gardens

Nephrolepis Exaltata
Sword Fern

Boston Fern is known to Northerners and Midwesterners as a hanging basket plant. In the North and Mid West, Boston Fern is an annual that dies when the weather gets colder. In the South it is called Sword Fern and grows as an evergreen. Sword Fern gives the Southern shade garden lush green foliage year round. Transplanted Southerners are surprised to learn that they are the same plant.

Nephrolepis Exaltata

Nerium Oleander
Olealder

Hero, in a Greek mythological story, is the handmaiden of Aphrodite. Hero spent her days up in a tower overlooking the river Hellespont, a river that divides Greece from Turkey. It was Hero's task to look beautiful and to attract the attention of a young prince whom she could marry. It wasn't long before Leander, a young prince from the Turkish side of the Hellespont, took notice of the beautiful Hero. Day after day he courted her and sang her love songs as she swooned in her tower.

After a while, Leander got tired of only looking at Hero and he decided to cross the river to pursue her. One night, while under the cover of darkness, Leander crossed the river with great concupiscence. As fate would have it, a tempest brewed up over the water that night and dashed young Leander's body against the rocks.

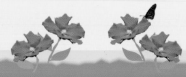

In the morning Hero went looking for her lost love. She walked up and down the banks of the Hellespont looking for him, and crying out "Oh, Leander"! Soon Hero found his dead and broken body on the shore. Clutched in his hand was an Oleander flower. Heartbroken, she took it back to her garden where she planted it and it grew, showing that their love still thrives even today.

Nerium Oleander

Oenothera
Evening Primrose

A simple garden flower, Evening Primrose is of timeless beauty and simplicity. Evening Primrose opens in the evening, welcoming people home at the end of a long day. Oenothera also comes in white and yellow varieties. A garden flower here in Savannah, Evening Primrose is a wildflower in the West, where it covers fields in Colorado and Utah.

Oenothera

Loquat oddity

Agapanthus oddity

Paeoniaceae
Peony

Peony is a beautiful May flowering perennial that is rare in Savannah, but would be familiar to New England and Mid Western gardeners. Typically it is too hot and humid in Savannah to grow Peonies reliably, but there are several nice specimens in the Historic District. Peonies are native to southern Europe and Asia.

A Chinese botanist spent his life caring for the Peony plant. He had spent so many years in the company of the Peony that he had no friends or family left, as time went on, he became in need of an employee to help him care for his growing collection of flowers.

As luck would have it, a beautiful young girl knocked on his door and asked if she could work for him. The botanist was happy to employ her and teach her the ways of the Peony. She was, as it turned out, a perfect student. The girl was quick to learn and of impeccable character, morally honorable and dedicated to both the botanist and the Peony collection.

Paeoniaceae

One day, a long lost love of the botanists came to the door for a visit. Wanting to introduce the woman to the young pupil, the botanist called to the student, and when she did not answer, went looking for her, but could not find her. He went into the greenhouse to search for her and found her flat against the wall hiding behind a piece of glass. No longer in human form, but now a painting, the young girl said to the botanist, "I did not answer you for I am no longer human, but have become the soul of the Peony". The girl in the painting continued "Your love warmed me into a human and it has been my joy to serve you, but you now have a real human to love and you no longer need me. Enjoy me as a flower, care for me as your own, but go and love her with all your heart". As the moments passed, the botanist's heart both broke and grew. He returned to his door. With tears of sadness and joy he invited the woman in. The botanist knew when the woman said "I love you. I've missed you terribly and I'm glad to be back with you and your beautiful Peony collection" that the young girl was right to return to the flowers.

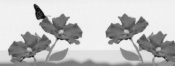

Paeoniaceae

Parkinsonia
Jerusalem Thorn or Mexican Palo Verde

Mexican Palo Verde tree is the state tree of Arizona, but grows here in the Southeast as well. Mexican Palo Verde produces a medium sized bright yellow flower in mid spring that nearly covers the tree. The branches of the Palo Verde bare short but wicked thorns along with leaves that are slender and lacy, giving Savannah's sub tropical climate a desert tree. Parkinsonia is considered invasive in some parts of Australia.

Jerusalem Thorn grows in Israel which is where the common name comes from. According to a Christian legend, this is the tree that was used to make the crown of thorns placed on the head of Jesus at the time of the crucifixion.

One version of this story says that Jerusalem Thorn branches were bunched together to make the whip that was used to flog Jesus, and then the whip was made into the crown of thorns.

Parkinsonia

Parkinsonia

Parthenocissus Quinquefolia
Virginia Creeper

This wonderful sprawling vine is all over Savannah, in some cases literally. Virginia Creeper provides Savannah some of its best fall color, turning shades of red, orange and yellow. Virginia Creeper and its cousin Boston Ivy cover many of the buildings on the college campuses of Yale, Harvard, Brown and Princeton, hence the name "The Ivy League."

Parthenocissus

Passiflora
Passion Vine

Passiflora is one of the most stunning flowers that can be seen in the Southeastern United States, including Savannah. The Passion Vine has a spectacular circular flower that looks like a floral space ship with its stamen set rising out of the center.

The name Passion does not refer to love in this case, but to the Passion of Christianity. Centuries ago, Christian missionaries discovered Passion Vine with its unique flower and saw in it symbols of Christianity. The crooked radial filaments represent the Crown of Thorns, especially in the red varieties.

Passiflora

The three stigma represent the Trinity and the lower five anthers represent the five wounds. The Passion Vine flower has been referred to by this symbolism throughout Christendom.

Passion Vine is the birthday flower for June 22nd. Passiflora fruit can be purchased at local roadside stands or neighborhood grocery stores under the name Passionfruit.

Petunia
Petunia

Petunia is a long-time favorite in gardens and hanging baskets all over America. Botanically Tobacco, Tomato, Potato, and Petunia are all related, as they are in the family Solanaceae. The home gardener has several sizes and colors from which to choose, including white, pink, red or purple as well as several variegated types.

Petunia

Philodendron
Philodendron

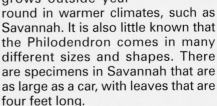

Philodendron, frequently mistaken for Pothos, is a popular houseplant all over America and Europe. It is commonly seen in large lobbies and waiting rooms as a foliage plant. Because of the way it is displayed, people do not realize that it actually grows outside year round in warmer climates, such as Savannah. It is also little known that the Philodendron comes in many different sizes and shapes. There are specimens in Savannah that are as large as a car, with leaves that are four feet long.

Philodendron

Philodendron gets its common name from two Latin words: philo, meaning brotherly love, and dendron, meaning tree. The Latin name literally means "tree love" or "tree of love." Dendrology is the scientific name for the study of trees.

Phoenix Canariensis
Canary Island Date Palm

In the oases of Saudi Arabia, the Date Palm stand tall with their fronds outstretched towards the sky and their roots anchored deep into the earth. These dense green groves have been a treasured part of the Saudi landscape for generations, both for their beauty and their utility. Since ancient times, the Date Palm has been a source of food for the people of the Arabian Peninsula, and its branches have granted them shade from the brutal desert sun. The palm fronds have thatched the roofs of their huts and provided the baskets in which they have gathered the savory and nutritious fruit that grows abundantly from this palm.

Phoenix

During Ramadan, the annual month of fasting for Muslims, the daily fast is broken with a few dates and sips of water. The end of Ramadan is celebrated with a four day feast, called Eid Al-Fitr. During this feast, a popular treat is a small cookie with a date filling called ma'mul.

The Date Palm is especially important to Saudis, not only for its many uses, but as a national symbol. After the modern kingdom was founded in 1932, the Date Palm was adopted as its national emblem, representing vitality and growth. The Date Palm continues to be an integral part of Saudi culture. Low in fat, cholesterol free, high in carbohydrates, fiber, potassium and vitamins, dates stay fresh for several weeks when properly stored. They are a delicious and nutritious part of the Saudi diet and an excellent source of energy. Canary Island Date Palms grow well all over Savannah, although very slowly.

Photinia
Red Tip

Photinia is a native shrub in the American Southeast and would once have been used by plantation owners to line the borders of their property. A large, thick evergreen shrub, Photinia forms an impenetrable hedge. It was used as a barrier plant to keep out unwanted thieves from plantations.

The common name, Red Tip, is from the new growth that comes out red in the spring before maturing to a deep olive green.

Red Tip is a disappearing shrub in Savannah. Several years ago, Red Tips got a disease that no one could cure and it wiped out Red Tips across the South. Once there were thousands of Photinias across Savannah, now only a few dozen remain. A similar shrub, Cleyera, has become the replacement plant in the landscape industry.

Photinia

Cleyera

Pinus Palustris
Longneedle Pine or Longleaf Pine

Longleaf Pine is native to the Southeastern United States. Longleaf Pine is much shorter and with a thicker trunk than its relative, the Loblolly Pine. Because it withstands storms, Longleaf Pine is a better choice for home landscape.

Commercially, Longleaf Pine is valuable for its long needles that are sold as pine needle mulch. Throughout the South many ornamental garden beds are lined with needles from the Longleaf Pine.

Pinus Palustris

Pinus Taeda
Loblolly Pine

Savannah was a pine grove when the explorer Oglethorpe arrived here in 1733. The Loblolly Pine can still be seen growing across Savannah and throughout the South. This Pine symbolizes the South in many ways, growing from Kentucky to Florida and from Georgia to Texas.

For many years the logging industry has depended on the Loblolly Pine, the tallest of the Southern Pines, to produce products ranging from turpentine and furniture to lumber for flooring.

The cone and branches of the Loblolly Pine have also been utilized in the arts and craft trade, for use as a table decoration at Thanksgiving and for strands of garland at Christmas.

While Loblolly Pines are a good industrial tree, many landscapers discourage homeowners from putting them in the residential landscape because of their tendency to break during storms and cause damage to cars and houses.

Pinus Taeda

Pittosporum Tobira
Pittosporum or Clown Plant

It is well known that professional clowns always round off the edges of their facepaint, so that sharp points around the mouth and eyes do not scare children. This idea is where Pittosporum gets its common name Clown Plant. Clown Plant has no thorns and soft rounded leaves that often curve slightly backward, giving this shrub a soft billowy form. Pittosporum makes a wonderful safe landscape shrub, especially where children or families play.

One other feature of this evergreen shrub is that it can come in a variegated form, which means it has a two toned leaf color. But be warned, Pittosporum's natural color is all green and in time a variegated form will revert back to its all green state. There are several examples of this transformation around Savannah, with a single plant having both all green and variegated leaves on the same shrub.

Pittosporum Tobira

Pleopeltis Polypodioides
Resurrection Fern

The Resurrection Fern is the weather vain of Ferns. It can tell the weather, in reverse at least. During dry spells, this fern goes dormant and appears to be dead. When rain comes, the water resurrects this fern making it fresh and green again. This is where Pleopeltis gets the common name Resurrection Fern. Despite the name Resurrection, this fern is one of the local Rabbi's favorite plants.

Don't look for Resurrection fern on the ground or in a flower bed. Resurrection Fern forms a short carpet of green fronds along the branches of the Live Oak and Sweet Gum trees. With a tongue twisting scientific name like Pleopeltis Polypodioides, Resurrection fern could not take itself too seriously.

Pleopeltis - flourishing

Pleopeltis - dormant

Chatterbox, a Savannah wildflower

Pteridophyta
Woodland Fern

Woodland Ferns include many varieties and are seen growing in many different habitats all over the world. Ferns are one of the oldest plants on the planet. They date back thousands of years. Differing from many other well known garden plants, ferns do not flower. They reproduce by spores that grow on the back of the frond. Whether choosing a large or small fern, they make a fun addition to any Savannah shade garden.

Pteridophyta

Punica Granatum
Pomegranate

The Pomegranate is featured in countless folklore stories throughout world history. According to Turkish folklore, a Pomegranate was the symbol of marriage. The blood red flower symbolized virginity, a gift given to the Groom. The fruit symbolized the womb and motherhood, and so, during her wedding, the Bride held up a Pomegranate for the guests to see and then threw it against the earth, smashing it. The Pomegranate fruit has many seeds and a bride wished for as many seeds to fall out as the fruit contained. She was to have a child for each of the seeds of the Pomegranate that fell loose on the ground.

Jewish tradition teaches that the Pomegranate is a symbol for righteousness, because it is said to have 613 seeds which coincides with the 613 mitzvot or commandments of the Torah. For this reason, many Jews eat Pomegranates on Rosh Hashanah and Sukkot.

Punica Granatum

Historic District porch planting

Quercus Virginiana
Live Oak

Who can come to Savannah and not be enchanted by the Live Oak's majestic size and unparalleled beauty? Live Oak is the massive tree one sees all over the Historic District. It has an open, irregular form with long branches that loom out over the roads, adding to Savannah's Southern charm.

Live Oaks produce a hard and extremely strong wood. Despite its strength, it is not a popular wood with woodworkers since the twisted branches and often leaning trunks have curved grains. Almost all modern woodworkers prefer straight grained woods. By these woodworking standards, Live Oak is typically considered unusable.

Quercus Virginiana in Johnson Square

However, in Savannah's early colonial days, shipbuilders actually grew groves of Live Oaks specifically for the unique curved grain structure of this native tree. The grain along a curved branch or trunk gave the shipbuilders special pieces of wood they called Arc Timbers. Arc Timbers formed the frame and hull of the ship. They had names such as futtocks, transoms, knees, flowers, and catts. In fact, shipbuilders would cut down an entire Live Oak just to get a single Arc Timber.

Shipbuilders sought out the trees looking for angles and bends that would produce the best of each Arc Timber needed. Depending upon the ship being built, Arc Timbers might number into the hundreds of pieces per ship. The pieces were cut following the grain of the wood. The curving flow of the grain gave the Arc Timbers their strength. A Live Oak frame was durable enough to handle the roughest seas and the heaviest of commercial ships. This Oak get's its common name, "Live Oak," because it is an evergreen and therefore looks "live" year round.

Quercus Virginiana allée at Wormsloe Plantation

Ratibida Peduncularis
Mexican Hat

Mexican Hat is native to the Southwestern United States into Mexico. Mexican Hat does well in Savannah, despite its being native to desert areas with low humidity. Ratibida is a Cone wildflower in the Echinacea family.

Ratibida Peduncularis

Rhaphiolepis Indica
Indian Hawthorne

Indian Hawthorne is a classic garden and landscape shrub in Savannah. Because Indian Hawthorne is low to the ground, it would have been readily accessible to Native Americans who would have used its berries to make a jam and it's wood to make tools. Today, this medium sized evergreen can be enjoyed for its abundant pink or white flowers. Rhaphiolepis has many landscape applications because it can be planted in the sun or in the shade.

Rhaphiolepis

Rhododendron
Azalea

Azalea is a classic old-fashion flowering shrub in Savannah. Azalea flowers, for many Southerners, are the first hint of spring. In early March the city of Savannah comes alive with color as red, white, pink, salmon, fuchsia and purple flowers enhance the vitality of the squares and gardens. Many Southerners who can not otherwise name a single shrub can identify an Azalea. Azalea festivals are a delight for locals and visitors alike. With the introduction of many new hybrids, Southerners can now enjoy a second display of fresh Azalea flowers in the fall as well. Azaleas are native to Japan, but there are some wild varieties native to North America. Northerners need not feel left out about Azaleas. The shrub Northerners call flowering Rhododendron is a close relative.

Rhododendron Azalea

106

Ricinus Communis
Castor

Despite its reputation for having an unpleasant taste, Castor oil is a very useful product often given to children to help with intestinal issues. Castor oil appears in many of the most common household products available today; everything from beauty products to motor oil.

The remainder of the Castor seed after oil production produces Ricin, a deadly toxin. It takes about 500 micrograms of Ricin for a lethal adult dose.

Castor make a wonderful garden plant with big tropical looking leaves and vibrant red seed sets. The Savannah gardener need only be mindful of its toxicity to safely enjoy this stunning tropical plant, native to Ethiopia.

Ricinus Communis

Rosa Banksaie
Lady Banks Rose

The Lady Banks Rose is truly a Southern garden favorite. Easy to grow, this sprawling rose falls gracefully across garden walls and fences. In Savannah and throughout the South it is often grown on and up through larger deciduous shrubs and trees so its early spring flowers can be enjoyed before the other leaves emerge.

Eudora Welty, a well known Southern writer, describes a Lady Banks Rose in the main character's family garden in the 1972 novel The Optimist's Daughter. Such a magnificent rose it is, that it should be carried in ones memory forever.

Rosa Banksiae

Rosmarinus Officinalis
Rosemary

Rosemary, a medium sized woody, evergreen herb with pungent Fir like leaves is native to the Mediterranean region. It is in the mint family, which also includes several other herbs. Rosmarinus does produce a small blue flower that is often overlooked in favor of other attributes.

Fresh and dried Rosemary leaves are used as an herb frequently in traditional Mediterranean cuisine. Rosemary, because of its strong, distinctive flavor and nutritional value, is extensively used in cooking throughout the world.

The ancient Romans used Rosemary for decoration, as well as for ceremonial occasions. Rosemary was frequently used as a headdress and garland for weddings or other special occasions. The cultures of the Mediterranean also used Rosemary in funeral rites, believing that the smoke

Rosmarinus Officinalis

would ward off demons that might try to invade earth through the bodies of the dead. It was also thought that by burning the branches, the rising smoke might help send the spirit of the deceased off into the heavens.

Rudbeckia and Dianthus
Black-Eyed Susan and Sweet William

These two old fashioned garden flowers have a romantic tale in common, told in "Black-eyed Susan", an old English poem by John Gay: "All in the Downs the fleet was moor'd, The streamers waving in the wind, When black-eyed Susan came aboard; 'O! Where shall I my true-love find? Tell me, ye jovial sailors, tell me true if my Sweet William sails among the crew.'"

This search for Sweet William is one of this garden flowers' tales, and adroit gardeners note that these two species are both biennials, bloom near the same time, and look wonderful together. The botanical name Dianthus is from the Greek words dios (god) and anthos (flower), meaning "God's flower" and was mentioned by the Greek naturalist Theophrastus.

Rudbeckia with Dianthus
in the background

Ruellia
Wild Petunia, Mexican Petunia, or Mary's Flower

Ruellia gets it's common name Petunia because it looks like a garden Petunia, although it is not a true Petunia at all. It is more closely related to Justicia Umbrosa, Brazilian Plume. Wild Petunia grows well in Savannah and is common here, thriving in hot and humid gardens.

Mexican Petunia can be seen growing wild over many parts of Mexico and that is where another common name, Mary's Flower, comes from. Mary's Flower can be seen growing in abundance outside of the many Catholic cathedrals and parish churches that dot the Mexican landscape. In the Christian tradition purple has been seen as a royal color, a color signifying the majesty of Christ. Mary's Flower, with its bright purple flower color, has for many years been cut and brought into the Cathedral sanctuaries to give to Mary, the Mother of Jesus.

Ruellia

Sabal Palmetto
Cabbage Palm or Sabal Palm

Pop quiz! There are fifty states in America, but there are only forty-eight state trees. Do you know which two states in America do not have a state tree?

No, it's not Georgia. It's our two neighboring states, Florida to the south and South Carolina to the north. The Sabal Palmetto is the state tree of both South Carolina and Florida. The truth is it's a bit of a trick question. The palm tree, any palm tree, is not actually a tree at all. Palm trees are in the grass family. What we normally call a palm tree is one big blade of grass. So, the next time you are eating coconut crème pie or corn on the cob....you're actually eating grass seed.

Sabal Palmetto at the old Jewish Cemetery

Salvia
Salvia or Sage

Salvia, or Sage as it is often called, is one of the hardest working perennials in the Savannah garden. There are dozens of different types of Sage to choose from, tall to short with flower colors ranging from bright red to deep purple. Salvias are one of the toughest garden plants, withstanding drought and brutal heat with seeming ease. Many Salvias spread, so in future years there will be lots of Sages to swap with friends. Salvia is an herb with many culinary and medicinal uses that go back for centuries. The name Sage was used to describe religious leaders who used this herb during sacred rituals, and eventually the name came to be used for the plant itself. The botanical name Salvia comes from the Latin word Salvare, which means "to save" or "to heal".

Salvia

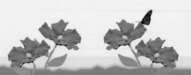

Schinus Terebinthifolius
Brazilian Pepper

Brazilian Pepper is known in Georgia as "The criminal tree". It is illegal to buy, sell or transport the Brazilian Pepper in Georgia, yet they are all over the place. Why is this? It is because the Brazilian Pepper is classified as an invasive plant. The joke in Savannah is you've got one... whether you want one or not.

Although the Brazilian Pepper is native to South America, it has been growing here since before the earliest colonists arrived. The Native Americans in this area harvested the berries, dried them and ground them into a Pepper style spice. Poisonous in large amounts, Brazilian Pepper berries are not true Peppers, but were often used in small quantities to season food.

Schinus

Sedum
Stonecrop

A lot of gardeners classify Sedum as a cactus, but it is not. It does require small but regular amounts of water. Sedum is a crassulaceae, making it a close relative of the familiar Jade plant.

Sedum

Strobilanthes
Persian Shield

Persian Shield, not known for its flower but for its coloration and leaf structure, is a most fascinating garden plant. Persian Shield captures the imagination with its motley leaves that have almost a metallic sheen. Strobilanthes is dominated by purple and silver, widely considered the most royal of colors. This plant is a favorite in Savannah gardens.

Persia is the historical name for the country we know today as Iran. A strange and intriguing story about the Persian Shield tells the tale of an ancient king who was guarded by an army of plants, named Persian Shield. The Persian Shield surrounded the king's palace, guarding him against anyone who would do him harm. Because of their extraordinary beauty and brilliant colors, the people of the empire wished to cut the leaves to take them home for their own gardens. However, the king saw this as a threat to his status and put a spell on

Strobilanthes

the Persian Shield; whoever cut the plant down would themselves be cut down. The irresistible beauty of the plant continued to draw those who would cut it for themselves, despite the curse. Eventually all of the plants were cut down, and the king himself was cut down along with the last of the Persian Shield. The king did not die, but grows today as the Persian Shield in gardens around the world.

Tagetes Lemmonii
Copper Canyon Daisy or Scent of Heaven

There are many things to love about the Copper Canyon Daisy. Scent of Heaven can be seen growing in several gardens around Savannah. The foliage fills the spring air with a rich fragrance that is unforgettable. Copper Canyon Daisy gets the common name Scent of Heaven because it is a plant that should be enjoyed as much for its heavenly scent as for its flowers.

Tagetes Lemmonii

This Texas native is very heat and drought tolerant, and has been grown successfully as far north as Charlotte, North Carolina. A Southern gardener wishing to plant a xeriscape flower bed that attracts butterflies should consider this late summer blooming shrub.

Copper Canyon Daisy is a relative of the Marigold. They have similar foliage and flowers, but unlike the Marigold, Copper Canyon Daisy is a reliable perennial, returning to be enjoyed year after year. Tagetes Lemmonii is Deer resistant.

Tetrapanax Papyriferum
Rice Paper Plant or Pith Paper

The plant that we call Rice Paper Plant in Savannah is known in other parts of the world as Pith Paper. It is a member of the Araliaceae family, which also includes Ginseng. It is native to China and Taiwan. A smooth, bone white paper has historically been made from the pith of the Tetrapanax Papyriferum plant.

In the eighteen hundreds, in China, the paper became popular as a medium for watercolor paintings. These paintings usually depicted scenes from daily life including plants, animals, landscapes and families. Pith paper became so popular in Chinese watercolor paintings, that even today it is available in high end art supply stores for reproductions of these watercolors. Pith paper has also been used to make artificial flowers and decorative articles in China, Japan and Korea for centuries. In Eastern Asia, the plant was referred to as "Tung-Tsao," meaning 'hollow plant.'

Tetrapanax Papyriferum

Tillandsia Usneoides
Spanish Moss or Grey Beard

Spanish Moss is the spooky looking gray plant that dangles down from the Live Oaks all over Savannah. Spanish Moss is a rather odd name given that it is neither Spanish nor Moss, but in the Bromeliad family Bromeliaceae. This family connection makes Spanish Moss related to both the popular houseplant Bromeliad and the Pineapple. Spanish Moss is featured prominently on the GreenFeet Walkabouts botanical tour of Savannah's Historic District.

Gorez Goz was a pirate from Florida, a mean and selfish brute. When he spied an Indian maiden, he made his concupiscent pursuit. Neither gold nor silver did Gorez want, but only the fair young girl. She, of course, wanted nothing to do

Tillandsia Usneoides

with the older, bearded man, and made her way to Savannah through the Live Oak limbs. She was small and nimble. He was big but strong, and so into the night the chase continued till it was nearly dawn. When at the banks of the river Savannah, the maiden made her leap, into the flowing water, free of Gorez Goz. The pirate with his beard all tangled could not continue the pursuit, and was left to dangle as Spanish Moss for all eternity. The original author of this story is unknown.

Trachelospermum Jasminoides
Star Jasmine or Trader's Compass

Trachelospermum Jasminoides is known by two common names. Star Jasmine gets its name from its fragrant white star shaped flower. Star Jasmine has a light fresh almost Gardenia like scent that swirls around the Savannah garden during the spring.

The other name, Trader's Compass, comes from Uzbekistan within it's native Eurasia. Hundreds of years ago trade routes crossed Uzbekistan, going from China to Old World Europe.

Trachelospermum Jasminoides

It was along these trade routes that the story of the Trader's Compass was found. A lost traveler could sit down and tell the Trader's Compass where they were going. If the Trader's Compass thought you were of noble character and up to good purposes, it would turn all of its leaves facing one way, pointing you in the right direction. However, if it thought you were up to nefarious purposes, it would turn all of its leaves in the wrong direction, thwarting your journey. Of course, if you were of questionable character, you would think that you had the ability to fool the plant, but, only the Trader's Compass knew. The moral of the story is to be of good character.

Tradescantia
Wandering Jew

The Wandering Jew is a figure from medieval Christian folklore whose legend began to spread in Europe in the thirteenth century. The original legend is about a Jew who taunted Jesus on the way to the Crucifixion and was, for his meanness, both blessed and cursed by Jesus to live and walk the earth forever.

Tradescantia gets its common name from the legend. Wandering Jew, much like the character in the story, lives and grows on every continent in the world. While Northerners know Wandering Jew as a potted plant, Southerners can grow it outside year round as a reliable perennial. Most often seen in purple, Savannah gardeners have either purple, white or blue flowers from which to choose.

Tradescantia

Troup Square

   Located along Habersham Street, Troup Square is seen here in all the lushness of mid-summer. Beautiful Troup Square is featured often on the GreenFeet Walkabouts tour for its diversity of plants and year-round color. Troup Square has magnificent Dogwood trees that have bracts in spring, as well as thriving Japanese Red Maples that add burgundy to the square's color palette. Several *Ginkgo Biloba* trees also grace Troup Square.

Troup Square in mid-summer

Verbena
Verbena

Verbena is grown as an ornamental plant in Savannah gardens, especially in xeriscape or reduced water gardens. Verbena comes in several colors such

as purple, pink or white. Verbena, while known mostly as a ground-cover, also comes in a branching upright stalk form with small lavender flowers at its tips. There are annual and perennial Verbenas.

Verbena has long been used by herbalists as a folk remedy, usually as an herbal brew. Some legends tell of Verbenas use as an herbal tea that was made to ward off Vampires. Still other tales tell of its association with Eos, the Greek goddess of the dawn. Verbena most likely got its association with Eos because its flower

Verbena

opens for the first time in the morning. In North American culture, they are the birthday flower for July 29th.

Vitex Agnus Castus
Chaste Tree, Chasteberry, or Monk's Pepper

In Greek mythology, *Vitex* flowers and leaves were used as an adornment during the festival of Cerius. Cerius was a Greek ceremony celebrating virginity and purity. For centuries, it has been believed to be an anti-aphrodisiac. For this reason Chasteberry is also commonly called Monk's Pepper because it was traditionally used as a libido suppression herb by monks to aid in their commitment to remain celibate. These stories are the origin of the common name Chaste Tree.

Vitex

Oddly, the berries of the *Vitex Agnus Castus* are also harvested for use in the equine or horse industry. The Chaste Tree berries produce an extract that has medicinal qualities that are used to reregulate hormones in mares after they have given birth. The Vitex berry extract is sometimes part of hormone therapy in human women after childbirth, and is sometimes prescribed for symptoms of menopause.

This dichotomy between celebrating virginity and its use in the childbirth process is quite fascinating.

Washingtonia Robusta
Mexican Fan Palm or California Skyrocket

Did you ever think that Los Angeles and Savannah had anything in common? California Skyrocket can be seen growing all over Los Angeles, especially along Rodeo Drive, where it lines the street in an almost magical allée of grandeur. This incredibly tall palm can also be seen growing throughout Savannah. Mexican Fan Palm is one of several palms that grow well along the Georgia coast and give the area its tropical feel.

Washingtonia Robusta

Yucca
Yucca or Spanish Bayonet

Savannah was originally settled as a buffer colony between the British in Charleston to the north and the Spaniards in Florida to the south. There were many battles between the British forces and the Spaniards along the Georgia coast and the need for weapons was immense. Sometimes a soldier might lose his bayonet in battle, and the Spaniards quickly discovered that they could use the Yucca, with its dagger like leaves and sharp point on the tip as a bayonet replacement, hence the common name Spanish Bayonet. Yuccas were also used without a rifle, simply as a blade style weapon.

The Yucca flower, which is always white, rises on a spike out of the center of whirled leaves in the late spring and persists into summer.

Yucca

Zinnia
Zinnia

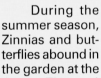

During the summer season, Zinnias and butterflies abound in the garden at the Owens-Thomas House. Zinnia is the most heat resistant flower in the Savannah border, looking beautiful even at the end of a long hot summer. These flowers come in many brilliant colors to brighten the garden.

Zinnia

Location Guide to Savannah Gardens and Plants

House Museum
Gardens in the Historic District

1. **Juliette Gordon Low Birthplace**; 10 E. Oglethorpe Ave.
   – Agave and Pomegranates
2. **Green Meldrim House**; 14 W. Macon St.
   – English style and Container Garden
3. **Mercer Williams House**; 429 Bull St.
   – Pindo Palm and Scuppernongs
4. **Owen-Thomas House**; 124 Abercorn St.
   – Common Fig and Hibiscus

Squares and Parks of the Historic District

Lafayette Square
   – Loropetalums and Animaginary
Chippewa Square
   – Azaleas
Troup Square
   – Azaleas and Magnolias
Oglethorpe Square
   – Mulberry Tree and Lily of Good Hope
Telfair Square
   – Sabal Palmettos, Camellias and Common Myrtle
Whitefield Square
   – Zinnias, Philodendrons and Peonies
Forsyth Park
   – Lantana and a variety of hardwood trees
Colonial Park Cemetery
   – wall ferns and Chinese Firs
Trustees Garden
   – The garden of the original Savannah Colonists

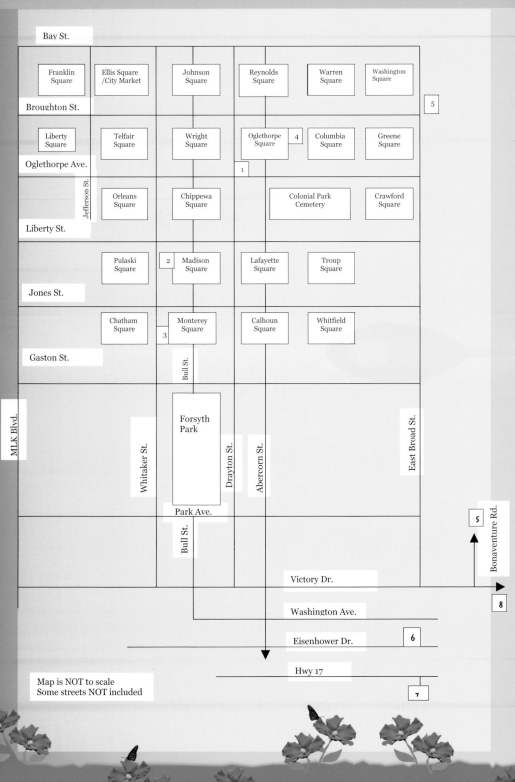

Bay St.

Franklin Square
Ellis Square /City Market
Johnson Square
Reynolds Square
Warren Square
Washington Square

5

Broughton St.

Liberty Square
Telfair Square
Wright Square
Oglethorpe Square
4
Columbia Square
Greene Square

Oglethorpe Ave.

1

Jefferson St.

Orleans Square
Chippewa Square
Colonial Park Cemetery
Crawford Square

Liberty St.

Pulaski Square
2
Madison Square
Lafayette Square
Troup Square

Jones St.

Chatham Square
3
Monterey Square
Calhoun Square
Whitfield Square

Gaston St.

Bull St.

MLK Blvd.

Forsyth Park

Whitaker St.

Drayton St.

Abercorn St.

East Broad St.

Park Ave.

Bull St.

5

Bonaventure Rd.

Victory Dr.

8

Washington Ave.

Eisenhower Dr.
6

Hwy 17

Map is NOT to scale
Some streets NOT included

7

Gardens Outside the Historic District

5. Bonaventure Cemetery

   features many graveside plantings
6. Savannah Botanical Gardens 1388 Eisenhower Dr.
7. Bamboo Farms and Coastal Gardens 2 Canebrake Rd. (Abercorn St. South to Hwy. 17)
8. Tybee Island
   features many seaside plants and flowers

Public Street Gardens

Washington Avenue in Ardsley Park
Jefferson Street
Jones Street
City Market
   – container gardens

Holly Tone - acid
Holly Plant - evergreen

Index of Common Plant Names

Cabbage Palm or **Sabal Palm**- *Sabal Palmetto* (Evergreen), 110

California Poppy or **Poppy**- *Eschscholzia Californica* (Summer), 43

California Skyrocket or **Mexican Fan Palm**- *Washingtonia Robusta* (Evergreen), 118

Canary Island Date Palm- *Phoenix Canariensis* (Evergreen), 92

Canna- *Cannaceae* (Spring into Summer), 23

Cast Iron Plant- *Aspidistra Elatior* (Evergreen), 16

Castor- *Ricinus Communis* (Summer into Fall), 107

Century Plant or **American Aloe**- *Agave* (Spring into Fall), 10

Camel Palm, European Fan Palm, or **Mediterranean Fan Palm**- *Chamaerops Humilis* (Evergreen), 26

Chameleon Plant or **Fish Mint**- *Houttuynia Cordata* (Summer into Fall), 117

Chaste Tree, Chasteberry or Monk's Pepper- *Vitex Agnus Castus* (Spring into Fall), 117

Chinese Fir or **Cunninghamia**- *Cunninghamia Lanceolata* (Evergreen), 34

Chinese Horned Holly or **Christmas Holly**- *Ilex Cornuta Rotunda* (Evergreen), 62

Christmas Holly or **Chinese Horned Holly**- *Ilex Cornuta Rotunda* (Evergreen), 62

Christmas Star or **Poinsettia**- *Euphorbia* (Fall into Winter), 43

Clematis or **Traveler's Joy**- *Clematis* (Summer), 29

Clown or **Plant Pittosporum**- *Pittosporum Tobira* (Evergreen), 97

Common Fig- *Ficus Carica* (Summer), 46

Common Myrtle- *Myrtus Communis* (Spring into Fall), 81

Copper Canyon Daisy or **Scent of Heaven**- *Tagetes Lemmonii* (Summer), 112

Coral Bean- *Erythrina* (Spring into Summer), 42

Crape Myrtle- *Lagerstroemia Indica* (Year Round), 72

Creeping Fig- *Ficus Pumila* (Evergreen), 47

Crinum Lily- *Crinum* (Summer), 30

Croton or **Milon of Croton**- *Codiaeum* (Evergreen), 31

Cunninghamia or **Chinese Fir**- *Cunninghamia Lanceolata* (Evergreen), 34

Daylily- *Hemerocallis* (Summer), 55

Devil's Backbone- *Euphorbia or Pedilanthus* (Evergreen), 44

Dioon or **Giant Sago Palm**- *Cycad* (Evergreen), 36

English Ivy- *Hedera Helex* (Evergreen), 53

Evening Primrose- *Oenothera* (Spring into Summer), 85

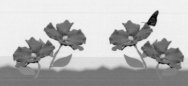

Lady Banks Rose- *Rosa Banksaie* (Spring into Summer), 107
Lantana- *Lantana Camara* (Spring into Summer), 74
Lily- *Lilium Asiaticum* (Spring), 76
Lily of the Incas, Princess Lily, or **Inca Lily**- *Alstroemeria* (Summer), 13
Lilly Turf or **Monkey Grass** *Liriope* (Evergreen), 76
Live Oak- *Quercus Virginiana* (Evergreen), 103
Loblolly Pine- *Pinus Taeda* (Evergreen), 96
Longneedle Pine or **Longleaf Pine**- *Pinus Palustris* (Evergreen), 95
Loquat- *Eriobotrya Japonica* (Year Round), 42
Lotus, **Bean of India** or **Sacred Lotus**- *Nelumbo Nucifera* (Summer), 82

Maidenhair or **The Dinosaur Tree**- *Ginkgo Biloba* (Spring into Fall), 51
Mary's Flower, Wild Petunia or **Mexican Petunia**- *Ruellia* (Spring into Fall), 109
Mediterranean Fan Palm, Camel Palm, or **European Fan Palm**- *Chamaerops Humilis* (Evergreen), 26
Mexican Bird of Paradise- *Caesalpinia Mexicana* (Spring into Summer), 22
Mexican Fan Palm or **California Skyrocket**- *Washingtonia Robusta* (Evergreen), 118
Mexican Hat- *Ratibida Peduncularis* (Summer), 105
Mexican Palo Verde or **Jerusalem Thorn**- *Parkinsonia* (Summer into Fall), 89
Mexican Petunia, Wild Petunia or **Mary's Flower**- *Ruellia* (Spring into Fall), 109
Milon of Croton or **Croton**- *Codiaeum* (Evergreen), 31
Mimosa Tree or **Tree of Beauty and Perseverance**- *Albizia Julibrissin* (Spring into Summer), 11
Monkey Grass or **Lilly Turf**- *Liriope* (Evergreen), 76
Monk's Pepper, Chaste Tree, or **Chasteberry**- *Vitex Agnus Castus* (Spring into Fall), 117
Mother of Millions or **Alien Cactus**- *Kalanchoe* (Spring into Summer), 72
Motley Mouth or **Snapdragons**- *Antirrhinum* (Winter), 15
Mulberry- *Morus* (Spring into Summer), 78
Mum- *Chrysanthemum* (Fall), 27

Oleander- *Nerium Oleander* (Spring into Fall), 84

Papyrus Plant or **Sedge**- *Cyperus Papyrus* (Evergreen), 37
Passion Vine- *Passiflora* (Summer), 90
Peony- *Paeoniaceae* (Spring), 87
Persian Shield- *Strobilanthes* (Summer), 112

night Blooming ~~Serious~~ big cerious

Sugi or **Japanese Cryptomeria**- *Cryptomeria* (Evergreen) 31

Summer Lilac or **Butterfly Shrub**- *Buddleja* (Summer), 19

Sunflower- *Helianthus* (Summer), 54

Sweet William and **Black-Eyed Susan**- *Rudbeckia* and *Dianthus* (Spring into Summer), 108

Sword Fern- *Nephrolepis Exaltata* (Evergreen), 84

The Dinosaur Tree or **Maidenhair**- *Ginkgo Biloba* (Spring into Fall), 51

Thomasville Citrangequat- *Citrus Poncirus Trifoliata x Citrus Sinensis x Fortunella* (Summer), 28

Tomochichi's Lantern or **Flowering Maple-** *Abutilon* (Spring into Fall), 7

Torture Juniper or **Hollywood Juniper**- *Juniperus Chinensis 'Torulosa'* (Evergreen), 71

Trader's Compass or **Star Jasmine**- *Trachelospermum Jasminoides* (Spring into Winter), 114

Traveler's Joy or **Clematis**- *Clematis* (Summer), 29

Tree of Beauty and Perseverance or **Mimosa Tree**- *Albizia Julibrissin* (Spring into Summer), 11

Tropical Hibiscus or **Hibiscus**- *Hibiscus* (Summer into Fall), 57

Verbena- *Verbena* (Spring into Summer), 117

Virginia Creeper- *Parthenocissus Quinquefolia* (Summer into Winter), 90

Wandering Jew- *Tradescantia* (Spring into Fall), 115

Wax Myrtle or **Bayberry**- *Myrica Cerifera* (Evergreen), 80

Wild Petunia, **Mexican Petunia** or **Mary's Flower**- *Ruellia* (Spring into Fall), 109

Witch Hazel or **Fringe Flower**- *Loropetalum* (Evergreen), 77

Woodbine or **Honeysuckle**- *Lonicera* (Year Round), 77

Woodland Fern- *Pteridophyta* (Evergreen), 100

Yarrow or **Soldiers' Woundwort**- *Achillea* (Spring into Summer), 9

Yucca or **Spanish Bayonet**- *Yucca* (Evergreen), 119

Zinnia- *Zinnia* (Summer into Winter), 119

Sage

Salvia